BOOZE

The drinks bible for the 21st century

RICHARD NEILL

CASSELL&CO

DEDICATION

To the memory of my dad – we'll have that drink someday.

First published in the United Kingdom
in 2001 by Cassell & Co

A CIP catalogue record for this book is available from the British Library.

ISBN 0304 356417

Illustrations: David Eldridge
Design: The Senate
Managing Editor: Hilary Lumsden
Editor: Jamie Ambrose

Printed and bound by L.E.G.O in Italy

Cassell & Co
Wellington House
125 Strand
London WC2R 0BB

contents

Why you need this book

Whether you think it's good for you (in moderation, of course) or bad for you (in which case my sales pitch is a little wasted), there is no denying that booze is more fashionable today than it has ever been.

Wine has slipped off its élitist shackles to become the favourite drink of the health-conscious, ciabatta-chomping masses. Beer has left the traditional realm of British Toby jugs behind and is showing off a bunch of far sexier outfits, while spirits have largely shaken off their old 'boozer' associations to become the favourite accessories of the 'badge-drinking' (or brand-following), style-bar hopper.

Meanwhile, new drinks now receive the sort of launch parties you'd normally associate with the fashion and music world and bars have become the new clubs. Not to be outdone, bartenders everywhere have done the old reinventionist's trick and emerged from the smoke as 'mixologists'.

No question about it: today, booze is news. Nine years ago – when I

began writing on this subject – the extent of my drink knowledge went something like this: wine came in red or white, beer was flat or fizzy, spirits were strong, and cocktails came with strange, eye-threatening garnishes. Oh, yes: and if you mixed grain and grape, your hangover would be twice as bad. Well, that's what my mum said, anyway.

It didn't take long to discover that the subject was as wide as an Oliver Reed grin. You only need to walk down the drinks aisle of any supermarket, scan the shelves of a good bar, or visit a beer or wine festival to realize that booze is far harder to learn about than it is to say or drink. There's your New World and your Old World, your top-fermented and your bottom-fermented, your double or triple distillation, your shaken vs stirred.

If there were a degree course called 'the knowledge of drink', it would take a couple of terms just to sip your way through the syllabus. Sure, there are plenty of drink books out there, but most are so dry in tone you need a drink just to make them digestible. More importantly, few are aimed at the nomadic novice drinker who might sup a wheat beer one night, a glass of Shiraz the next and a nip of Scotch the night after. So first and foremost, I wanted *Booze* to offer a good basic grounding in all areas of the bar list.

Secondly, it had to be as easy (and fun) to read as it is to drink – that's why I called it *Booze* rather than 'Beer, Wine, Spirits, Cocktails and all the alcoholic bits in between'. Thirdly, it needed to be practical. Most people just want guidance on what to drink, what flavours they can expect when they drink it, how to drink it, and how to get over the hangover when they drink too much of it. By reading this book, you will (hopefully) become a more informed drinker. With that knowledge will come the confidence to jump off your normal buying tracks and veer into the far corners of the global drinks cabinet.

With wine you'll find out how to choose it, buy it, taste it, save it, invest in it and even (providing you are suitably connected) surf the web for it. Moving on to spirits, whether your tipple is a single-estate rum, a sipping Tequila or bison-grass vodka, *Booze* takes all the facts and jargon and distils them into a series of neat shots of essential information. Making it, tasting it, drinking it, experiencing it, mixing it – read on and you'll never have to ask the barman an embarrassing question again.

Then, having found out how to make some of the best new cocktails, you'll move onto the brewing department and discover the difference between mild and bitter, between stout and porter, and between real lager and not-so-real lager. And finally, you'll be shown how to pick the right booze for every situation – whether it's a picnic, a wedding, a hot date or a student party on a slim budget.

What this book won't do is make you fluent in booze – you'll have to practise at the bar to reach that level. However, it will help you get past the line in the phrase book that says 'Just the usual, please'. Happy drinking.

The history of booze (the abridged version)

BC

- Prehistoric man relieves the tedium of rock painting by eating partially fermented fruits left out in the sun.
- According to Genesis 9:20, 'Noah began the planting of vineyards'. Presumably this was a distraction from zoo-keeping duties.
- Drinking vessels discovered along the Silk Route suggest beer was being drunk and traded up to 5,000 years ago. Excavations in Iran date wine-drinking back to as early as 5000BC.
- The first forms of distillation can be traced to early perfume-makers. Early drunks were obviously known for their sweet-smelling breath.

AD

1000–1100

- Benedictine monks of Salerno distil spirits with herbs, spices and berries. The first gin prototype is created in the monastery kitchen.

1100–1400

- Vodka appears sometime in the 12th century. Early attempts were probably made from rye and – being on the crude end of the distillation scale – were responsible for a few deaths as well as hangovers.

- In medieval Europe, beer is the most popular beverage. At a penny for two gallons, you can buy a good session with your mates and still have change for a cart-ride home.

1400–1600

- First written records of whisky production in Scotland and vodka in Poland. The number of new spirits being born (and consumed) at this time suggests early versions of the FTSE suffer major slumps.
- A bunch of Germans unintentionally create the first lagers by storing their beer in icy caves over winter.

1600s

- Unimpressed by the quality of some French wine imports, the English inject bubbles into it at least 30 years before the Champenois make their own fizz.
- The Thirty Years' War comes to an end. British soldiers return home with the recipe for a Dutch spirit called genever. British gin is born.
- The monks are at it again. This time it's the Carthusians, and their contribution to God's great booze cabinet is Chartreuse.
- First versions of the modern wine bottle appear, allowing wine

exports to take off. At around the same time, wine glasses appear.

1700s
• Settlers arrive in Kentucky and Tennessee and begin distilling rye whiskey. Gin production in England peaks at 20 million gallons.
• Don José Antonio Cuervo is granted land to farm agave in the Jalisco region of Mexico, and the beginnings of a Tequila industry take shape.
• The first patented corkscrew goes on sale.
• Porter and stout sales take off in Britain.

1800s
• Absinthe becomes the favourite tipple of the bourgeoisie. By mid-century, the French are drinking more of 'the green fairy' than brandy.
• Phylloxera sweeps across European vineyards and dozens of redundant French winemakers head off to South America to make wine.
• The Australian wine industry splutters to a start.
• The 1855 Bordeaux Classification is created.
• The word 'cocktail' first appears in an American dictionary. The first cocktail book is published in 1862.

• German immigrants arrive in Milwaukee. Using their knowledge of bottom-fermenting technology and ice from nearby lakes, they begin brewing the first American lagers.

1900–1940
• A great sobering-up period begins. Absinthe is banned by the French government in 1915; its less-potent cousin Pernod takes its place.
• In 1919, Sweden places the production and sale of alcohol under control of a state monopoly.
• Prohibition in Russia lasts from 1914–25 and in the US from 1920–33. Bootleg booze industries thrive.

1940s
• The Second World War brings widespread destruction of vineyards and some great stories of booze evacuations. Just before the Nazis invade the Crimea, Stalin orders the entire Massandra wine collection moved to safety. The winemakers of Hungary aren't so lucky: stocks of Tokáji are severely hammered by a thirsty Russian army.

1950s
• An Australian winemaker called Max Schubert returns from a trip

to Bordeaux and begins making an experimental wine called Penfolds Grange. The reputation of New World wine is changed forever.
• Vodka sales take off in the US, and the world's first airport duty-free liquor store opens at Shannon in the Republic of Ireland.

1960s
• Bacardi is forced to move out of Cuba and relocate production to Puerto Rico after Fidel Castro nationalizes spirit production.
• Draught lager is introduced into UK pubs, and drinkers react by creating a beer cocktail called the 'lager top'.
• Robert Mondavi launches the first new Napa Valley winery since Prohibition. Table wine at last out-sells fortified sweet wine in America.

1970s
• The decade of big hair, big trousers and big discos is also the decade that Robert Parker starts publishing *The Wine Advocate* magazine in the US. The world's most powerful wine critic is up and running; premium wine will never be the same again.
• The arrival of cheap foreign travel and package holidays helps introduce millions of Northern Europeans to wine (and lager).
• In response to the decline of British cask-conditioned beer, four beer-drinking friends set up the Campaign for Real Ale (CAMRA).
• In the US, a microbrewery movement begins on the West Coast.

1980s
• Terrible music, terrible clothes and some terrible drinks make their mark on a decade of excess. 'Sex on the Beach' and 'Brain Haemorrhages' are the cocktails of the day, Champagne sales soar as yuppies everywhere celebrate making money, and designer lagers like Sapporo start a 'badge-drinking' trend.
• Australian winemaker Nigel Sneyd flies to France to make some wine for a British mail-order firm; the term 'flying winemaker' is coined.
• New Zealand Sauvignon Blanc bursts onto the wine scene.
• Australian Chardonnay spearheads the beginnings of a New World wine boom.
• Guinness develops a small plastic mechanism (the widget) that allows it to replicate draught Guinness in a can or bottle.

1990s

• Australian farmer Duncan MacGillivray turns an unforeseen lemon glut into a new fermented drink; the alcopop is born.
By 1996, sales of 'alcoholic carbonates' reach 74 million bottles a year in Britain alone.

• Inventor Dennis Burns patents the silicon cork. Today, over 100 million Supremecorqs are made every year; traditional corks face increasing competition from a growing band of synthetic closures.

• New World wines are the fashion to bring to dinner parties; brands become the new châteaux. Jacob's Creek becomes a phenomenal Australian export success, and supermarkets take wine out of its élitist niche and bring it to a willing mass market.

• Château Pétrus puts invisible dots on its wine label as a precaution against rising wine fraud.

• After resurfacing in the bars of Prague, absinthe becomes the first-choice anaesthetic for a new generation of bohemians in search of rhapsody. At the same time, cocktails come back into fashion and the Martini is reinvented in a variety of flavoured ways.

• Two researchers at Glasgow University discover that Chilean Cabernet Sauvignon seems to have the highest levels of antioxidants. New research continues to suggest that red wine (and beer and whisky) can be good for you if drunk in moderation.

• In April 1996, a Hong Kong buyer pays £7,000 for a double magnum of 1982 Le Pin. During the same month, a Singaporean spends over £130,000 on various lots of the same baby Pomerol property. Other small-production *garagiste* producers begin to command ridiculously high prices, spawning a new generation of cult wines.

• Wine joins the dotcom party. The online wine shop becomes a reality.

2000 and on

• The world wakes up from its post-millennium hangover, drinks a large post-millennium Bloody Mary and says, 'Right, what shall I drink next?'

• Wine becomes the new beer, beer tries to reinvent itself as the new wine, and spirits just battle with each other for prime position in the latest style bar.

• Booze has never been more fashionable than it is today.

The future of booze

Booze 2025: a drink odyssey

• Global warming has caused a major reshuffling of the world wine order. Southern England and Germany begin to make world-beating Chardonnay. Southern Spain has become a desert.

• Lack of water and high saline concentrations in the soil cause thousands of acres of Australian vineyard to die. Fosters is now made with desalinated seawater.

• The permitted use of genetically modified vines allows Germans to start making Australian-style reds in the Mosel and Algerians to make delicate desert-grown Rieslings. GM lagers are made with special yeasts that create a longer-lasting head.

• In expanded mosquito-infested areas, the gin & (quinine-boosted) tonic makes a major comeback.

• Following the success of boutique wineries and microbreweries, mini-distilleries become the latest fashion.

• The number of vodka brands increases to such an extent that bars start employing vodka sommeliers.

• Jacob's Creek and Gallo are now produced under licence around the world and wine brands now account for 90 percent of the market. The other 10 percent (boutique stuff) are so expensive that no one dares to drink them. The CWSE (Cult Wine Stock Exchange) results appear daily in the newspapers.

• There is such a depth of scientific evidence that red wine is good for you that bottles carry 'flavonol content' messages on their labels. Cabernet Sauvignon tablets become the bestselling dietary supplement.

• Following the success of Greg Norman Wines, celebrity-endorsed drinks (or 'icon-assisted' as they are known in marketing circles) are everywhere. Tiger Tinto is the golfer's favourite 19th-hole tipple, and Harry Potter's Mysterious Cocktails are the bestselling pre-mixed drinks in the world.

• Drinks with lots of flavour are back in fashion. Lager sales plummet; in an attempt to stop the rot, one of the major lager manufacturers launches a range of flavoured lagers. British Real Ales are back in demand. Brewers allow their cask-conditioned ales to be brewed under licence in other countries. Fuller's London Pride is made in Shanghai, Sydney and São Paulo.

• Bartenders (or mixologists, as they were called at the turn of the millennium) have been replaced by machines that make perfect cocktails without trying to chat up customers or asking for ridiculously inflated appearance fees.

• Thanks to WAP-phone technology, sommeliers also become obsolete. Customers download prices and critical ratings of all the wines on a restaurant list and make their choices accordingly.

• As a result of the new 24-hour society, daytime parties (for those working the night shifts) become the most fashionable social events.

• Just as the last English pub is turned into a theme bar, someone decides that the next theme should be the classic English Pub.

• Oak forests are now so rare and wood shortages so severe that wine and spirits can no longer be matured in barrels. Unoaked wines and white spirits become the norm.

• The arrival of the computer-driven car means drink-driving laws become obsolete; alcohol consumption rises. Post-prandials like port and Cognac come back into fashion.

• A wealthy entrepreneur buys what remains of the ice cap and bottles it as it melts. Polar Water becomes the most expensive and fashionable mineral water on the market.

• Robert Parker – the world's most powerful wine critic – retires and hands over the reins to an unknown successor who is rumoured to like white wine more than red. A frenzy of replanting occurs around the world.

• As the world's top wines become more and more expensive, forgeries increase. Invisible 'fake-breaking' codes and holograms are the norm on bottles of claret and burgundy.

• A new hangover-preventing drug is developed, but government fears over worldwide inebriation cause it to be banned immediately.

Booze personalities

THE CONNOISSEUR

The Connoisseur treats all drink with the greatest of respect – it is never referred to as booze. Wine is always fine wine, beer is always real ale and whisky is always single malt. Connoisseurs are very easy to spot because they hold their glasses by the stems, keep their drinks in their mouths far longer than anyone else, and have a curious habit of writing notes at the dinner table.

UNLIKELY TO SAY:
'Down in one.'

THE LOUT

The complete antithesis of the Connoisseur, the Lout believes in quantity, not quality. Although he (for the Lout is invariably a he) is just as passionate about the art of imbibing, his interest lies in the effects rather than the taste. Lager is his fuel of choice, with spirits used merely as a booster to help catch up with the crowd. Totally non-PC in his views, the Lout believes wine is 'for the ladies'.

UNLIKELY TO SAY:
'Do I detect a slight hoppy edge to this beer?'

THE SERIOUS DRINKER

This character frequents every bar and every party, usually jabbering away to no one in particular about issues like *terroir* and the fact that a pint of beer is never a full pint. The Serious Drinker has a rather sad ability to remember facts and figures about drink; no matter what the product is, you can bet: a) it doesn't taste as good as it used to, and b) a conspiracy theory lurks somewhere.

UNLIKELY TO SAY:
'Cheers, mate. Next round on me?'

THE BON VIVEUR

Every family, every bunch of mates, and every party has a Bon Viveur lurking in its midst. You'll find this individual propping up the bar (and the atmosphere) wherever you go. No matter when you see him, he'll have a full glass in his hand and a stack of new jokes in his head. He doesn't mind what he drinks, worries about the next round, not the next hangover, and seems to have a tab wherever he goes.

UNLIKELY TO SAY:
'Better drink up: I've got to go.'

THE ADVENTURER

Always in search of the latest taste experience, the Adventurer prefers the obscure and idiosyncratic drink to the widely available big-brand labels. If there's a new beer on tap, a strange wine on the list, or a bizarre liqueur behind the counter, the Adventurer will feel compelled to try it. Easily identified standing by the booze cabinet full of strange concoctions picked up in duty free.

UNLIKELY TO SAY:
'The usual, please.'

THE SAFE DRINKER

If you had to delegate one friend to give your cellar a complete makeover, this person would be bottom of the list. There are two types of Safe Drinker. At the cheap end, there are those who buy nothing but well-known brands, always look for Chardonnay, and invariably take their favourite brand of spirit on holiday. And at the expensive end, the Safe Drinker only buys something if it has a high critic's rating.

UNLIKELY TO SAY:
'I'll let you choose.'

THE BUDGET BOOZER

Price is everything to the Budget Boozer. Permanently stuck on the lower rungs of the price-point ladder, Budget Boozers cruise the supermarket shelves, searching for cheap deals and bargains. The Budget Boozer drinks nothing but house wine, duty-free spirits, and cans of beer with 25 percent extra. And if things get really bad, there's always homebrew to fall back on.

UNLIKELY TO SAY:
'Do you think I should decant this?'

THE BLUE-CHIP DRINKER

Life is extremely good for this élite crowd. With no financial restrictions, the Blue-Chip Drinkers collect the world's finest wines and spirits and treat booze like they do stocks and shares. They're happy to be seen discussing it, reading about it, and (in the privacy of their own cellars) perhaps even fondling it, yet you'll rarely see them drinking it. Like the Safe Drinker, they stick to a predictable list of 'must-have' labels.

UNLIKELY TO SAY:
'When did you say the sale starts?'

The seven ages of booze

First encounter

The timing of booze baptism varies enormously from culture to culture and from family to family. If your parents are vineyard owners in southern Italy, you'll probably be drinking a few drops of *vino rosso* with your mother's milk. If your parents are a couple of Amish schoolteachers living in an isolated rural hamlet, it's going to take some initiative to lose your alcoholic cherry. Either way, your first drink – which invariably will be cheap and sweet – is highly likely to leave you with a profound sense of nausea and a guaranteed ride on the bed-spin express.

Experimentation

Having discovered the effects of this magic potion, your next move will most probably be to go through a crucial period of trial and error (ie, you will try it all and make lots of errors). Alcopops, Martini Rosso, scrumpy cider, quarter bottles of cheap whisky, lager shandy, homebrew – by the time you have reached 18, there is a good chance you will have completed the full chamber of drinking horrors. It may seem

a rather crude form of booze exposure, but it's all part of the process of natural conditioning. Hopefully your body will never allow you to stoop so low again.

Student daze

During this important period of education, the booze student will tend to steer down the quantitative rather than the qualitative path. Important skills such as coordination (carrying trays of drinks), vocal harmony (beer-drinking songs), financial juggling (running a bar tab off a student loan) and rehydration management (dealing with hangovers) have to be learned fast. More than anything else, the student is a master of the economics of booze – name a drink and he or she will know the price.

The TFI Friday phase

Having graduated with honours from Booze University, the inevitable requirement to get a job means a change in drinking patterns. Even with a steady supply of Red Bull in your top desk drawer, you will now be forced to fit your booze around your working life. Apart from the occasional weekday 'one for the road', most of your consumption will be concentrated into the Big Friday Night Binge. Bottled lager, energy drinks mixed with vodka, cocktails and New World Chardonnay... these are the staples of the 20-something office worker.

The golden years

Somewhere between growing out of the TFI Friday stage and reaching the garden-shed years there is a glorious (but, sadly, short) window of opportunity for quality drinking. You now have the right amount of money to start buying decent gear and the right attitude to start appreciating its finer points. For once, you actually peruse a wine list with the intent of buying something rather than just filling in time before ordering the house plonk. You discover microbrewed beers, single-estate rums, sipping Tequilas and the joy of life outside branded wines. You begin to talk about drinks rather than just use drinks to help your talk.

The family unit

Onto the road of the mature, responsible adult and with the last true hangover a receding memory, you have moved to the drinking-less-but-better phase. Here, booze appreciation has switched from what it does to your head and confidence to what it does to your heart and soul. Quaffing has been replaced by sipping, New World by Old World, lager by ale, and fashionable spirits by beautiful but deeply unfashionable spirits. You've reached the 'habits and hobbies' stage of life. You lay down more wine than you drink, you consider buying *en primeur* rather than asking what it is, and you stop drinking outside mealtimes.

Retirement tippling

The circle completes itself. You'll find that, just as you started this alcoholic learning curve on a sweet note, so you'll end it on one. Medium-sweet sherry, off-dry wines, liqueurs, port... these are the staples of the retirement home booze cupboard. At a time when you need a drink the most, you don't even have the strength to get the cork out of the bottle. With luck, however, there will be a sympathetic staff-member or relative willing to help you out.

The big boom

There was a time when wine was just something your parents did. Apart from that little sip the vicar gave you to unglue the dry wafer on your tongue, contact with fermented grape juice came only when someone pressed your 'mature adult' button and decreed that you were grown-up enough to give it a go.

There was also a time when wine was nothing more than an intimidating, jargon-riddled subject studied by appellation control freaks who talked about the stuff more than they drank it. To join the club you had to have graduated from the Wine Blurb School of Daft Language and shown suitable geological qualifications to the *terroir* police at the door. Wine was élitist, snobbish, overcomplicated and about as accessible as the tradesmen's entrance to The White House.

Today, thankfully, that situation no longer exists. It doesn't matter who you are, what you earn or what you know, the door to Club Wine is now wide open and there is no dress code or request for references. Now you can know zilch about wine but still choose something off the shelves. You can be on a student budget but still buy something that tastes nice. You can be in the middle of nowhere but still find a bottle of Chardonnay. The wine snobs haven't all gone away, but the new democracy of the bottle shop has left them looking like an increasingly irrelevant and powerless bunch.

Along with this newly acquired popularity, a lot of good things have happened to wine. It has become a lot cheaper (and expensive), a lot less frightening, a lot more fashionable (cult wines are the new rich man's dining accessory), a lot easier to buy and a lot easier to drink (everything is softer).

But the really good news is that while wine has shaken off its bad associations, it hasn't lost the positive attributes that make it the most fascinating and challenging drink in the world. It is still a drink that can express a sense of origin and originality like no other, a drink that can develop with time like no other, a drink that can linger on the memory like no other, and a drink that can inspire like no other.

Buying it

Before deciding what colour, style, and price of wine you want, you first need to choose the place you want to buy it. Assuming you don't live in an Islamic state or a country where distribution is still controlled by a government monopoly, there should be plenty of options available. In what is still very much a traditional industry – with more middlemen and lengthy lunches than any other trade – the arrival of wine-on-the-web has been as much of a shock to some as the use of the words 'efficiency' and 'speed' in the same sentence. Personally, I welcome the arrival of the virtual bottle store, but I hope there will always be a place for the dusty old wine shop and the guy in the apron who recognizes your tastes as fast as your face. In an age of high stress and fast living, buying wine from a real rather than virtual face is the best bit of shopping therapy you can get.

TEN WAYS TO BUY YOUR WINE

Winery back door
If you happen to live in a wine-producing country, one of the nicest (and often cheapest) ways to stock up your cellar is to drive around and buy directly from the producer of your choice. You can usually taste before you buy and put some faces to the names on the labels.

Supermarkets
Hundreds of wines, cheap prices, reliable brands and not a single wine snob in sight – the aisles might sometimes be crowded, but this is the wine retailing of choice for those on a budget and a tight time schedule.

Independent wine merchants
Once upon a time, this is where everyone came to buy wine. Today, it still makes for a brand-free shopping experience for those who prefer to keep their wet goods separate from their dry goods.

Discount clubs

Join one of the big cash 'n' carry operations and you might be surprised at how good the wine selection is and how big the price reductions are.

Auctions

Mid-shoulder, slightly scuffed label, stored in original cases, one good owner. If you want old claret, burgundy, port or some old Champagne someone found in a shipwreck, you might just have to bid for it.

Brokers

Just as there are blue-chip stocks, so there are blue-chip wines – and groups of people who make a reasonable living out of buying and selling wine with just a computer, a phone, and a good memory for vintages and prices.

Mail order

If you live in the country, and getting to your local wine shop requires organizing an overland expedition (or if you just can't be bothered to get out of your chair), buying by brochure is a good option.

Off the web

Wine is now only a computer screen away, and you can do everything from bidding for top claret, selling part of your cellar or ordering your wedding wine without much more effort than a few swipes of the mouse.

In a restaurant

This is probably the most intimidating and expensive place to buy wine, thanks to a combination of unhelpful wine lists (*see* 'How to deal with a restaurant wine list', page 38), snobbish wine waiters and often extortionate mark-ups.

Duty free

Most people associate duty free with spirits, but anyone who has visited the Berry Brothers shops at Heathrow International Airport will know that there are some brilliant bargains to be found. Just make sure that Lafite doesn't get smashed in transit – and if you're heading for countries such as the United States or any of the Arabic nations, make sure you know what (if any) the allowances are.

Supermarkets vs independents

SUPERMARKETS

Supermarkets (well, those that sell booze at any rate) offer the most convenient and least intimidating way of buying a bottle of wine. Here is wine retailing in its most accessible, unpretentious and uncomplicated state.

Having negotiated the great zig-zag course to the wine aisle, all you need do is steer your heavily laden chariot down the 30-metre stretch of bottles and pluck out what you want as you pass by. There's no one around to make you feel embarrassed about any lack of knowledge, there's a lot of simple sign-posting, lots of recognizable labels, and lots of very attractive prices. It's wine-buying made easy, and whatever you think of these giant grocers, you can't deny that they've helped introduce this beverage to an entirely new audience and improved the quality of basic quaffing material beyond recognition.

That's the good news. Now for the not-so-good. Look a bit closer at those ranks of upright bottles and you'll notice a familiar ring to the names on the labels. Unless you've become completely immune to discountitis, you might wonder why so many of the wines in front of you are on special offer or feature cut-price deals. The reason is simple: big supermarkets naturally like to keep one step ahead of their big neighbours, and they can only do this if they offer big bargains. And where is it easiest to offer big bargains? Why, in big-brand land, of course.

What does this mean for you, the wine-drinker? Well, if you're happy drinking uncomplicated, good-value wines that deliver the same consistency and reliability you get from your favourite brand of washing powder, then it means that you are shopping in precisely the right place. If you like New World wines (increasingly favoured by supermarkets), then stay where you are. But if there's even an ounce of Indiana Jones in your wine-buying character, you will soon need to beat a path past all those familiar ridges, creeks and gullies to find some geography that wasn't dreamed up in a marketing department.

LIFE BEYOND THE TROLLEY

Eventually, you'll summon up all your retailing courage and make the bold move of buying your wine outside a supermarket. Straight away, this means you are dedicating some individual shopping time to vino rather than just squeezing it in between finding a loaf of bread and finding a place in queue number 26. And because the enjoyment of something is directly related to the time and effort invested in choosing it, your drinking pleasure is about to increase immeasurably.

Your first step away from trolley-buying will probably be in one of the wine-shop chains. The brands and discounts will still be here, but you will also be able to find a good range of more idiosyncratic wines made on a scale that prevents them gaining entry into the supermarkets. Here is where the personal service kicks in. Despite the fact that staff turnover is often fast in these chains, you should be able to begin building a relationship with someone who will be your link to wines that fit your taste.

The second and bolder step – and not nearly so easy a transition to make as step number one – is to find a good independent wine merchant. Somewhere near to where you live will be a bunch of people who specialize in the weird, the wonderful, and the 'we'd better get a decanter for this' type of wine. This is where you can discover wines that taste of places rather than price points, members of the grape family you never knew existed, odd regions, great vineyards, obscure cooperatives, eccentric wine producers, and a cast of different vintages.

To help you through this maze, there will be mailing lists filled with passionate prose, knowledgeable staff who provide professional wine-guidance counselling, and wine-tasting events where you can take a new wine out for a test drive and see how it handles before putting down the readies. Once you get used to this sort of service (and wine), I doubt very much that you'll ever set foot in a supermarket wine aisle again.

Choosing your wine by price

Style, mood, ingredients, label design, and even alcohol content can draw the drinker to a particular bottle, but ultimately (unless you are a recent lottery winner) it is price that determines what consumers eventually pluck off the shelves.

Taking into account we all have different perceptions of what is value for money and what is an overpriced joke, where do you get most bang for your buck these days and what is the difference between premium and plonk?

From the cheap wine you will usually find on special offer in the supermarket right up to the mega-priced, heavyweight bottle on the top shelf of the most exclusive wine shop, the guide below will lead you up the price-point ladder and show you exactly what you can expect for your money at each rung.

£3 and under: the 'trying to end a relationship' wine

If you take out all the fixed costs (labels, corks, duty, etc) of the winemaking process, you'll find that, at this price point, the value of the stuff in the bottle is barely the same as that of a tin of baked beans. Apart from wetting the tongue, providing some innocuously flavoured alcohol and helping lubricate a meal, these bargain-basement bottles will provide little in the way of drinking pleasure. If it tastes of oak, it's thanks to chips – not barrels – and if it has any sense of place to its character, that place is in the stew.

£3–£5: the 'single person's everyday drinking' wine

At this price, the wines start to have a single grape variety on the label and – more importantly – they start to have some distinctive flavours (wine buffs call it 'varietal character'). Being in the heart of big-brand country, these are basically manufactured 'formula' wines that are enjoyable but very forgettable. As you get closer to the crucial £5 mark, you'll begin to notice a gradual improvement in intensity, depth, texture and length of the wine, and you should also get a hint of (second-hand) barrel.

£5–£7.50: the 'trying to impress a first date' wine

You've now moved from cattle class to business class, and you only need to experience this sort of quality once to know a return to the cheap seats will be difficult indeed. At this price, the winemaker has had the time and money to put some real care and dedication into both the raw materials (old vines, French oak) and the winemaking. If it's value for money you want, then this is definitely where to come.

£7.50–£10: the 'meet the in-laws' wine

Another step up and you are now firmly in single-estate/barrel-select/special *cuvée* territory. The fruit is out of the best vineyards, the yeast is possibly wild rather than cultured, the oak in the barrels is from a top cooperage and the wine has been kept in bottle for a year before release. What you get for your extra money is structure, finesse, length and complexity.

£10–£30: the 'will you marry me' wine

Instead of a few extras thrown in, you should be getting all the perks here. At this price, you'll be drinking the best the New World can offer but still only the best of the second division from the Old World. These are wines that should have seen a bit of horizontal time before being opened, and the decanter might have to be dusted down and used for the first time.

Over £30: the 'lay something down for the baby' wine

Welcome to the world of small-production, handcrafted wines that taste of a particular patch of very special dirt (sorry, *terroir*). At this level, the price of a wine can be influenced by factors unrelated to quality. Fashion, winemaker ego, a good Robert Parker score, snob value, greed, machismo and rarity... one or all of these can cause an artificially inflated price that often bears little relation to the quality of the wine inside the bottle. Up in these lofty heights, the concept of value for money goes out the window, and in many ways you have to tread more carefully here (to avoid a major disappointment) than you do at the mid-price levels.

Scaling the price-point ladder

Premium brands
Move up a step and
you'll find the French
Connections and
Benettons. Better quality
and more style, but still
nothing very original
or surprising.

Cheap brands
Here we find the Gaps of
the wine world – reliable,
easy-wearing wines made
to a formula that appeals
to the masses. Many get
stuck on this plateau
of accessible flavour,
but boredom usually
nudges them on.

Bargain basement
The first rung on the wine
ladder and not one you
want to linger on for too
long. Home to bulk wine,
supermarket own-labels
and discounted stock.
It's wet, it's alcoholic
and it's cheap.

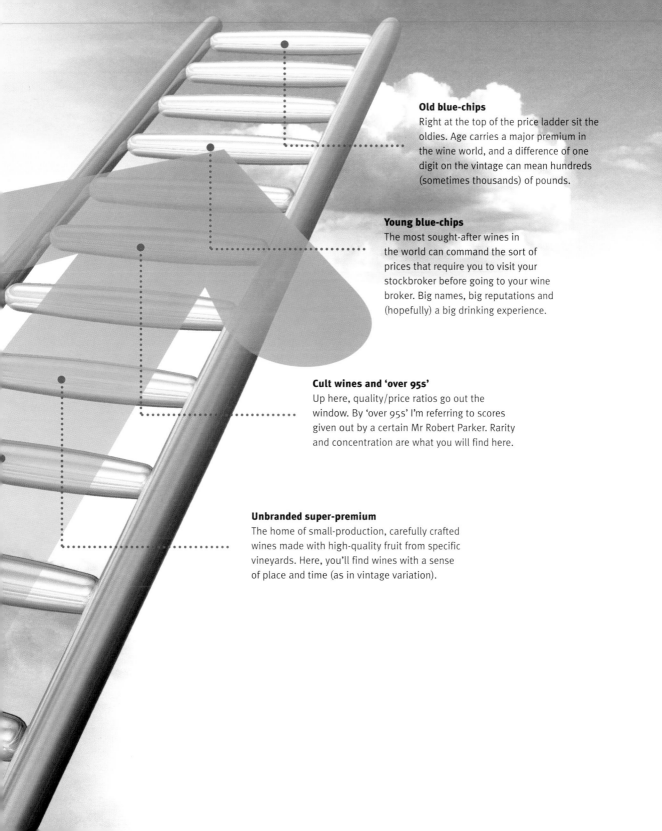

Old blue-chips
Right at the top of the price ladder sit the oldies. Age carries a major premium in the wine world, and a difference of one digit on the vintage can mean hundreds (sometimes thousands) of pounds.

Young blue-chips
The most sought-after wines in the world can command the sort of prices that require you to visit your stockbroker before going to your wine broker. Big names, big reputations and (hopefully) a big drinking experience.

Cult wines and 'over 95s'
Up here, quality/price ratios go out the window. By 'over 95s' I'm referring to scores given out by a certain Mr Robert Parker. Rarity and concentration are what you will find here.

Unbranded super-premium
The home of small-production, carefully crafted wines made with high-quality fruit from specific vineyards. Here, you'll find wines with a sense of place and time (as in vintage variation).

Buying wine off the web

Scene one

You're in a swanky restaurant and you've just tasted a great wine that you've never seen or tasted anywhere else. You take your WAP phone out of your pocket, log on to one of the wine websites, tap in the name of the wine, and bingo! Within minutes, you've found the stockist and ordered a case.

Scene two

You're in your office, sneaking a quick lunch-hour. While munching on a sandwich you log on to www.winebid.com and place a bid on a case of rather nice old burgundy. The following morning you receive an email informing you that your bid was successful.

Scene three

A small-production, cult-wine company decides that instead of using the normal distribution channels, it will sell all its stock by tender on its website. Hearing the news, you log on to the site, place your bid and, hey, you're on a lucky streak: you get six bottles of a wine most of your friends will never have tasted before.

These three situations might seem to lie in the realms of journalistic fantasy, but in fact they are all very real. The internet has and will continue to change the way we buy and sell wine. Even if you fail to get excited by the prospect of shopping in a virtual wine merchant's shop, it's hard not to be intrigued by the possibilities this medium brings to the way the world buys its wine.

Imagine being able to watch the first grapes being crushed at New Zealand's Cloudy Bay winery, live on your computer screen. In theory, it could mean a cheaper bottle of Sauvignon Blanc for you and me. And imagine if you could buy your case of classed-growth claret directly off the website of your château of choice: instead of coming to you via a *courtier* (two percent cut), a *négociant* (10 percent) and a broker (another 10 percent), you would be buying at the price the producer sets – which is bound to be much cheaper than at any wine shop.

Today, the question is no longer if or when, but rather how fast the internet economy will change the traditional structure of the wine industry. Many of the web's new start-ups may last no longer than a couple of vintages, but those that get speed, efficiency, choice and (most vital of all) distribution right will be around for the long haul. Just as with any internet business, delivery will be the key to success. After all, what is the point of buying your wine off the internet if it takes eight days or more for your order to turn up?

Those who prefer a non-virtual approach, however, shouldn't worry: however efficient and easy the internet wine trade becomes, the traditional 'bricks and mortar' wine shop is not about to be forced into extinction. Just as importers and retailers will still favour the long, lazy, wine-trade lunch over video conferences and email decision-making, there are bound to be many consumers who will still want the touchy-feely experience of browsing and buying in a place where there is human rather than cyber assistance.

WHAT YOU CAN DO ON THE WEB

- Buy wine at virtual auctions (www.winebid.com)
- Buy and sell at a fine-wine stock exchange (www.uvine.com)
- Visit a first-growth château (www.haut-brion.com)
- Track the price of your cellar over a 20-year period (www.decanter.com)
- Learn about a wine region (www.napavintners.com)
- Buy wine *en primeur* (www.bbr.com)
- Find out what wine goes with what food (www.wine-pages.com)
- Book a wine tour (www.winetours.co.uk)

FIVE SITES WORTH SURFING

1 Virginwines.com: The wine arm of Branson's empire is one of the most consumer-friendly sites.
2 Madaboutwine.com: from cellar planning to party oganizing, this is the most comprehensive site.
3 Decanter.com: with a superb archive of written material, this is a great site to learn more from.
4 Vine2wine.com: links to scores of wine sites, with great reviews.
5 Winesearcher.com: quick route to finding stockists and best prices.

The wine-on-the-web routefinder

Through the keyhole

www.cloudybay.co.nz

www.penfolds.com

www.moet.com

www.antinori.it

www.torres.es

www.lafite.com

www.ridgewine.com

www.mondavi.com

www.haut-brion.com

www.fetzer.com

Geography lessons

www.wineaustralia.com

www.wine.co.za

www.bordeaux-wine.com

www.languedoc-wines.com

www.nzwine.com

www.oregonwine.org

www.winesofchile.com

Virtual merchants

www.wine.com

www.wineplanet.com

www.madaboutwine.com

www.virginwines.com

www.chateauonline.com

www.winesmart.com

www.cybercellar.co.za

**Bidding, broking and
exchanging wine**

www.bordeauxindex.com

www.farr-vintners.com

www.uvine.com

www.winebid.com

www.christies.com

www.sothebys.com

www.langtons.com.au

www.cellarexchange.com

**Warning: e-commerce lifespans vary from site to site so sadly there is no guarantee that
all these names will be with us in the future.**

Clicks and bricks

www.bbr.com

www.oddbins.co.uk

www.laithwaites.co.uk

www.bibendum-wine.co.uk

www.corneyandbarrow.com

www.majestic.co.uk

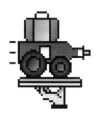

Sun, fun and fermentations

www.arblasterandclarke.com

www.winetours-france.com

www.tasteofthevine.co.uk

www.sources-caudalie.com

**Blind dates
(matching food and wine)**

www.wine-pages.com

www.decanter.com

www.foodandwine.co.nz

Media luvvies

www.decanter.com

www.winexwired.com

www.winespectator.com

www.wineadvocate.com

www.winetoday.com

www.wineenthusiast.com

Grape fanatics

www.zinfandel.org

www.oregonpinotnoir.com

www.pinotage.org

Finding wines

www.winesearcher.com

www.wineresearch.com

Wine gear

www.winebooks.co.uk

www.reidelcrystal.com

www.hclaccessories.com

How to deal with a restaurant wine list

COPING WITH WINELISTPHOBIA

Are you sitting comfortably? Okay, you may now open your examination paper. Pages one to three are for financially challenged students only, no assistance is allowed from those sitting close to you, and when the man in black returns to the table, your time is up.

Do you ever get the feeling that reading a restaurant wine list is a bit like sitting an examination? It felt that way to me when my editor took me out to lunch a few weeks after securing the wine-columnist post. Nervous of screwing up but not wishing to be seen as Mr Safe and Boring, I took a punt on a German Riesling and ended up suffering the embarrassment of having two bright-green Riesling goblets brought to the table. 'What the hell are these?' said my new boss, as the entire restaurant turned their attention to the two guys with the naff glasses.

Choosing wines in this environment is like picking the winner in an egg-and-spoon race. With a limited amount of wine knowledge, you – the one at the table who has been decreed 'the wine selector' – are required to wade through a list that resembles a till receipt and pick out something that suits your bank balance and everyone else's food. No wonder most people head for the nearest Chardonnay lifebuoy when faced by a heavily accented examination board (the sommelier).

But don't panic. By following some simple advice, you can keep wine-list trauma to a minimum and avoid turning a hot date into a cold sweat.

THE BLUFFER'S GUIDE TO WINE-LIST SURVIVAL

Set your own examination time

Don't feel pressurized into making a rapid decision. There is no time limit on when you have to choose a bottle, so try a wine by the glass first and select your main bottle when you've relaxed a bit.

Look for the recognizables

If you feel like you are in an exam, treat the list as you would an exam paper and look for things you recognize. Scan for wine producers and grape varieties you know you've tried before.

Know what's safe and what's risky

German Riesling (how sweet will it be?), mid-level Bordeaux (how good will it be?) and South African Pinotage (how weird will it be?) are all examples of risky wines. Chilean Merlot and New Zealand Sauvignon Blanc are, by comparison, safer bets and therefore better options in potentially embarrassing situations.

Watch out for those vintages

With inexpensive wines, going for the most recent vintage possible will at least guarantee a greater degree of freshness. For older stuff, use the sommelier's advice as a safety net; if it's bad, then at least you can blame someone else.

Don't assume price relates to quality

As a general rule, the correlation between price and vintage (whether 'on' or 'off') is much less clear in restaurants than it is in the shops. A higher price doesn't necessarily mean a better wine.

Head for food-friendly wines

Full-bodied, high-alcohol wines (did someone mention the New World?) might do well in wine competitions, but they aren't always the best at matching food. Medium-bodied reds (like Chianti) and neutral whites (Pinot Grigio) are better food wines.

Don't be afraid to send it back

If you think the wine is corked (*see* page 95) or if you are just not satisfied that the wine is as good as it should be, you are perfectly within your rights to ask for a replacement.

Try before you buy

If the restaurant offers a list of wines by the glass, ask for a tasting sample. Most places won't mind doing this if the bottle is already open.

Don't rule out the BYO option

These days, more restaurants than you think will allow you to bring your own wine for a set corkage charge. The result is a pressure-free meal with a wine that you know you really wanted to drink.

The bottle family

The burgundy bottle
A wider bottle with gently curved sides and no shoulders, this is the favoured shape for Chardonnay and Pinot Noir.

The airline bottle
A small, screw-cap affair invariably filled with something as distressing as the accompanying food.

The baby Champagne bottle (with optional straw)
A favourite in fashion-party circles, this offers both portability and an excuse to be a totally selfish drinker.

The half bottle
Great for the lunchtime drinker but a bit like the single person's baby loaf of bread: there is a stigma attached to having one of these in your trolley.

The claret bottle
Easily identifiable by its straight sides and shoulders, this is the classic Bordeaux packaging. Also used for claret-style reds from other parts of the world.

The Germanic bottle
This tall, thin, usually brown-coloured flute is associated with German wines and Riesling. Anyone using this bottle has immediately reduced his or her fashion status by three notches.

The underweight bottle
So light and thin, the contents will invariably weigh more than the container. This bottle is the mark of a cheap wine.

The sexy bottle
Loved by Italian winemakers, this usually has tapered sides, wide shoulders and an abyss-sized punt in the bottom. Watch out for the unsexy price.

The gimmicky bottle
Strange colours and shapes make this stand out from the crowd, but don't expect the contents to be as flash.

The overweight bottle
So thick and heavy it rarely breaks when thrown into the bottle bank, this is associated with the overpriced, premium wine.

The flange-top bottle
The Ford Capri of the bottle circuit, this lip-necked container is a favourite with New World wine producers. They (the bottles, not the producers) normally come with an annoying blob of wax on top of the cork.

The big bottle
Ideal for parties, this bottle family extends from magnums (two normal bottles) up to the Nebuchadnezzar (20 bottles).

The bottle-stopper family

Cheap cork

Agglomerated corks – all the bits that didn't make it into a premium cork get mashed up and glued together – are a pain in the neck (of the bottle). They're hard to get out, even harder to push back in, and they're liable to taint your wine whenever an opportunity arises.

Twin-top corks

Here we have the cork equivalent of a sandwich made with two nice bits of bread and a rather unsavoury filling. Two discs of decent quality are glued onto the ends of a cheaper middle section, the theory being that the wine only comes into contact with the good cork.

Expensive cork

These are far longer than their cheapo counterparts and a really good one will have very few holes and cavities in it. There is still a chance your £50 bottle will be ruined, but the odds are considerably lessened.

Synthetic corks

Supremecorq, Integra, Nomacorc, Betacorque... the names may be different, but the common aim is to provide a synthetic stopper that won't taint your wine like a piece of bark can. Ideal for wines destined to be drunk young, but it's too early to say how wine will age when bunged with one of these.

Screw cap

Associated with cheap wine, these twist-off caps are now being used for some expensive Australian white wines. Guaranteed to keep things fresh and taint-free, but there is still a massive stigma attached to opening your wine with a flick of the wrist.

Crown cap

A few wine producers are using the classic beer caps on their wine bottles. As well as having all the advantages of a screw cap, they look far more fashionable.

Label linguistics

Name of the producer

The absolutely
meaningless
marketing jargon

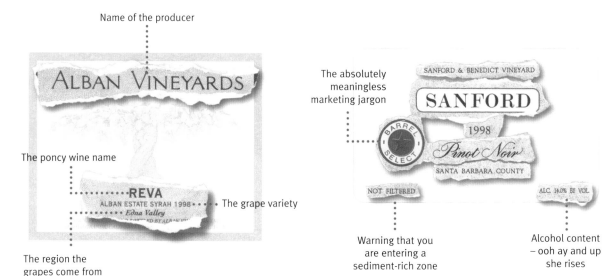

The poncy wine name

REVA
ALBAN ESTATE SYRAH 1998
Edna Valley

The grape variety

The region the
grapes come from

Warning that you
are entering a
sediment-rich zone

Alcohol content
– ooh ay and up
she rises

The strange warnings
that appear on all
American bottles.
Just who is this
Mr Surgeon anyway?

The poncy Italian
wine name

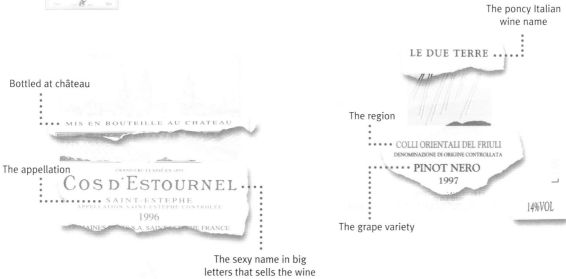

Bottled at château

MIS EN BOUTEILLE AU CHATEAU

The region

COLLI ORIENTALI DEL FRIULI
DENOMINAZIONE DI ORIGINE CONTROLLATA

The appellation

GRAND CRU CLASSÉ EN 1855

COS D'ESTOURNEL

SAINT-ESTEPHE
APPELLATION SAINT-ESTEPHE CONTROLÉE

1996

PINOT NERO
1997

14%VOL

The grape variety

The sexy name in big
letters that sells the wine

Label blurb – what it all means

FRONT LABELS

What started on the right note with New World varietal labelling (the grape variety being the biggest, boldest thing on the label) has headed into the land of confusion as more and more wine jargon has begun to appear on the front and back of bottles. Phrases like 'basket-pressed', 'wild yeast' and 'old vines' might sound impressive, but do they actually mean anything? Here, then, is label blurb unplugged.

Basket-pressed

This means the grapes have been squeezed in one of those old, wooden, cylindrical presses they used to use before modern, computer-controlled machines arrived. Winemakers claim basket presses offer a gentler method of releasing the juice, and because they also act as a filter, the juice is clearer as well. The cynic (that's me) wonders why, if they are so good, they were chucked out in the first place?

Family selection/classic/limited-release/show reserve

Out of the winery thesaurus has come an avalanche of terms that supposedly imply you are drinking a small-production, higher-quality wine. The truth is that these phrases crop up on many large-volume, commercial wines and they rarely guarantee a better product.

Old vines/*vieilles vignes*

This is probably the most used and abused of all viticultural marketing tags. The theory is that old vines produce smaller quantities of higher-quality fruit (and therefore better wine), and to a large degree this is true. But when does a vine become old? Because there is no legal definition of when the term 'old vine' can be used, there appear to be far more old-vine wines on the shelves than all the old vines in the world could create. Treat this term with some suspicion.

Single-estate/vineyard/block/row

A label term that signifies that the wine has been made from a select area of vines. Unfortunately, just like the lack of definition on vine age, there are no rules governing how big or small a vineyard has to be to warrant the tag 'single vineyard' on the label. It is also debatable whether a wine made from fruit from a single source is better than one made with grapes from different vineyards.

Unfiltered

This first started cropping up on California wine labels, but it is now appearing on bottles from all parts of the wine world. Despite what unfiltered supporters say ('solids make an important contribution to flavour'), it is impossible to prove that an unfiltered wine is better than a filtered one. If you see the word 'unfiltered' on a label, treat it only as a warning to decant.

BACK LABELS

Back labels are largely a New World invention – if you turn a French bottle around, you are still more than likely to find a blank space. In theory, the back label is there to give you extra information that will help you decide whether this is the bottle you want to buy. In reality, it is often little more than a clichéd sales pitch that tells you absolutely nothing.

Left on its lees

'Lees' are the dead yeast cells that fall to the bottom of the tank or barrel after fermentation. If you leave the wine in contact with these deposits (or even stir the deposits), you can add flavour and texture to a wine.

Fermented with wild yeast

Many winemakers prefer using wild (indigenous) yeast rather than cultured to ferment wine. It might produce a different style of wine, but not necessarily a better one.

Made using traditional techniques

Means the winery hasn't got around to investing in new equipment yet.

Made in a modern style

Means the wine probably tastes squeaky clean and faultless, but it could also taste utterly boring.

Made in the sun-drenched...

Back labels are always filled with geographical eulogies that mean absolutely nothing. Ignore the bits about clean rivers, fertile plains, etc.

Ideal with pasta, cheese and red meats

This food-and-wine-matching advice is so ubiquitous you wonder whether the entire winemaking community is eating the same thing.

Handy hints for budding wine investors

After the obvious 'where can I get a bargain?' requests, the most common question I am asked is, 'I've got this bottle in my cellar. Should I sell it?'

As the prices of the world's top wines have spiralled – particularly for a clutch of small-production cult wines – more and more people have been tempted to include wine in their investment portfolios. More worryingly, a growing number of bogus dealers have emerged to lure the gullible and naive with supposed 'great opportunities' on claret, port and Champagne.

Obviously, I'd much rather you bought wine to drink rather than to stash away as a nest egg, but I am here to serve, not judge. Here, then, are my tips for building a goldmine under the stairs.

Make sure you've got a lot of money and a lot of room under your stairs
The wines that usually sell for lots of money are the ones that cost a lot of money in the first place. And it therefore follows that the people who make profits on wine are usually those who have plenty of profit to spend.

Apply the following formula to your investment strategy
For every given wine, take the average Robert Parker score and divide by the total number of hectares of vineyard (rarity is as good a price guarantee as Parker points). The higher the figure you are left with, the greater the investment potential.

Keep a look out for potential new cult wines
If a talented, big-winery winemaker breaks away to set up his or her own small-scale operation, get yourself on the mailing list even if you haven't tasted the wine.

Build up a blue-chip portfolio
Demand for the world's most desirable wines (first growths, top burgundies and a handful of so-called 'garage wines') is always going to outstrip supply, so buy the best.

Start buying premium white wines
Fashion comes in cycles, and it

can't be long before red goes out of vogue and demand for white picks up. If you can persuade a top doctor to do some research on the healthy benefits of drinking white wine, this will boost your white-wine investment prospects enormously.

Put a little Vorsprung durch Technik into your cellar

The white wines that are still ridiculously undervalued (in relation to the amount of critical plaudits they receive) are top German Rieslings. As well as being good value for money, they age longer than just about any other wine on the planet.

Think long-term, think New World

Until recently, only a handful of New World premium wines have made appearances on auction catalogues, but as a younger generation of New World-loving wine-drinkers takes over from their claret-quaffing parents, so the balance is changing. Which means it's time to raid the southern hemisphere.

Avoid new, super-premium wines

Barely a week goes by without the launch of another new, super-premium wine in a bottle weighing more than your average dumb-bell. Almost without exception, these overpriced rarities have more style than substance, and rely on hype rather than reputation. Joint-venture wines are the guiltiest.

Don't put your investments in a damp place

Unlike those who buy wine and store it with the idea of drinking it later (a strange concept, I know), the investor should ensure the storage conditions are label-friendly more than wine-friendly. Japanese and American collectors have become notoriously picky about the state of the labels – in other words, mouldy Moutons are just not acceptable nowadays.

Buy at source

Here's an idea for a good year off from work. Buy yourself a temperature-controlled trailer and pay a visit to the best wineries in the world. Buying from the cellar door will save you money by cutting out all those middlemen margins.

Frank's second-hand wine dealership – learning the lingo

PUKKA PROVENANCE

The wine's previous owner(s) was a perfectly respectable gentleman and not some wheeler-dealer who refuses to say where the bottles came from.

LAVERLY... ORIGINAL TISSUE AND STRAW, MADAME

The wine is still in its original packaging and will be perfect for the collector who likes to look at (but not drink) his or her wine.

BOTTOM SHOULDER, but we'll do you a deal, squire

The level of the wine is at the low end of the bottle's shoulder, but we've reduced the price to compensate for the high risk of it being undrinkable.

GOOD ULLAGE, MY SON!

The level of the wine in the bottle suggests the cork and the wine are both in good nick.

1EB 2UK

One of these wines was estate-bottled and the other two were bottled in the United Kingdom.

REPACKAGED
FROM OWC

This wine is no longer in
its original wooden case
and you would be wise
to enquire why.

DAMP-AFFECTED
LABELS,
DARLIN

There's a bit of mould on the label,
but this would suggest the storage
conditions were perfect.

IT'S A BIT
BIN-SOILED
but trust us, guv
it's good gear

The labels are a bit on the
dirty side because the wine
has been stored in open
bins in the cellar.

RECONDITIONED

The wine has been re-labelled and
re-corked, and we believe it will be
in your best interests to find out
where this happened.

Second-hand dealers

BUYING OLD WINES

Like cars, wines can go through several owners. If you're thinking of buying an older vintage, you should a) choose a reputable second-hand dealer and b) make sure you look under the hood and check that your investment is in good order.

The two main outlets for buying second-hand wines (as in previously owned rather than previously drunk) are auction houses and wine brokers.

The auction-house route

Buying wine at auction can be exciting, but it is also very easy to get carried away and spend more than you need to. In addition, there is no guarantee that you will get what you came for, and – particularly if you are selling – it can be a long time between deciding to sell and actually receiving your money. Online auctioneers such as winebid.com are bringing greater speed, flexibility and accessibility to the house of hammer.

Going for brokerage

Wine brokers are basically nothing more than stockbrokers who deal in blue-chip wines rather than shares. If ever there was proof that *terroir* is an asset and wine is a highly tradeable commodity, you simply need to visit one of these companies and see the world of wine reduced to lists of châteaux, vintages and prices. Using a broker is a far speedier method of trading old, rare wines, for both the buyer and the seller. Another advantage is that there is no risk of you being outbid at the last minute.

A case for quality control

In both cases, checking the quality of the second-hand gear is a bit trickier. Although some auction houses do hold pre-sale tastings, normally you won't get the chance to give the wine a test-run. What you can do, though, is check up on who the previous owners were (storage conditions) and make judgments based on the fuel levels (ullage) and the condition of the bodywork (pristine or rotten labels). A 50-year-old wine with a low shoulder ullage level and a label in perfect condition is not something you'd want to buy in a hurry.

TEN BUYING TIPS FOR THE AUCTION VIRGIN

1 Do your homework before the auction. Ring around and check the going price for the wine you want to buy.

2 Set yourself a price limit before bidding begins.

3 Remember to read the small print on the auction catalogue. Don't forget that commission and VAT will be charged on top of the hammer price.

4 'No returns will be accepted' is the auction rule, so do your research and check the provenance of the wine before the big day.

5 Avoid heavily hyped celebrity sales. Publicity equals more bidders equals higher prices.

6 Be wary of the 11-bottle lot. The quality (or lack of) of that 12th bottle is probably the reason the owner is selling.

7 Avoid buying wine with low ullages – this is the best sign of bad storage conditions.

8 If you are buying to drink rather than to hoard, the best wines to buy are ones with perfect levels and soiled labels. A lot of American and Asian collectors will only buy wines with perfect labels – despite the fact that soiled labels suggest better storage conditions.

9 If there is a large parcel of wine with 20 lots containing a case each, hold your bid until the later lots. Generally, prices get cheaper as you go down the parcel.

10 Don't go looking for a bargain at a charity auction.

FAKE ALERT

Just as there is fake jewellery, art, and designer clothing, there is also a potentially lucrative market in dressing up a cheap wine in expensive clothes. While a few of the top châteaux have introduced anti-fake protection in their packaging (Château Pétrus, for example, has incorporated a random series of invisible dots on its labels), most rely on the vigilance of the wine trade to spot fraudulent bottles. If you are at all suspicious – for instance, the person selling to you refuses to divulge how or where he or she came by the wine – get an expert to give it a thorough examination.

Choosing it

Wine is the most chaotic, confusing, mentally challenging product on the shelves, and without assistance, the novice wine-drinker can soon end up looking like Jack Nicholson in that famous 'lost in the maze' scene. Cast adrift in a sea of mumbo-jumbo, the most natural reaction is to look for some sort of marker, and in this section I will focus on some simple coordinates to help cut through the fog.

The best starting point is to select the style of wine you want to drink; from there, you can pin things down further by choosing the ingredients (grape varieties), the destination (New World or Old World) and the level of risk (a brand or a little-known producer).

STYLES OF WINE

The neutral, refreshing ones

Dry, oak-free wines designed for quaffing rather than contemplative tasting. Ideal for summer BBQs, picnics and throw-it-together meals.
SHOPPING LIST: Italian (particularly Pinot Grigio) and English whites, Muscadet, Vinho Verde, Mâcon Blanc.

The aromatic, head-clearing ones

Extrovert wines that jump out of the glass, whizz up your nostrils and clear out the cobwebs in the grey area. Perfect wake-up material for brunches.
SHOPPING LIST: New Zealand Sauvignon Blanc, Argentine Torrontes, Muscat, German and Australian Riesling, Gewürztraminer.

The Chardonnay (and Chardonnay-ish) ones

Comforting, oak-aged reliables that feel as good as they taste. At the cheap end, these are collapse-in-a-sofa-type wines, and at the expensive end, they'll take your shoes off, give you a head massage and cook dinner.
SHOPPING LIST: New World Chardonnay, Semillon, Marsanne, Viognier, decent white burgundy.

The pink ones

The best-looking wines on the shelf are also the most unfashionable and underrated. Rosé is fun, refreshing, and very good at matching food.
SHOPPING LIST: Tavel, Anjou, Provence, Bordeaux: all make fabulous rosés.

The soft, juicy, red ones

A step up from rosé but a step down from medium-bodied reds, here is a range of light, fruity wines that you can bung in the fridge and drink chilled in summer or serve with delicate dishes in winter. Low on oak, high on fruit.

SHOPPING LIST: Beaujolais, Valpolicella, New World Merlot.

The big, blockbuster red ones

Full-bodied, concentrated carpet-scarers that come into their own during winter. Often rich, sometimes spicy, definitely oaky, these are big wines that need big glasses and big food. Think Jerry Bruckheimer, not Terence Mallick.

SHOPPING LIST: Barolo, Australian Shiraz, California Zinfandel, Chilean Cabernet, Châteauneuf-du-Pape.

The intellectual, arthouse red ones (with subtitles)

Wines that require thought before (decanting), during (drinking) and after (discussion) the performance. If you want subtlety and complexity, step this way for a beautiful but wallet-lightening experience.

SHOPPING LIST: Top Bordeaux and burgundy.

The fizzy ones

Celebrations, parties, weddings, ship-launching... all of these will require a wine that can spray froth everywhere. Fizzy wines come in all shapes, styles and prices, but no matter which one you open, jollification is guaranteed.

SHOPPING LIST: Champagne, sparkling wine.

The sticky ones

Sweet wines – or 'stickies', as the Aussies call them – are not everyone's cup of nectar, but you'd be daft to write them off as granny material. Personally, I think Sauternes should be available on prescription.

SHOPPING LIST: Sweet German Riesling, Sauternes and Barsac, vin santo, Tokáji, New World late-harvest wines.

The fortified ones

They may be considered as another fashion disaster area, but these spirit-boosted wines still offer some of the most extraordinary drinking experiences in the world. Smoking jackets, plummy accents and large stately homes are not required.

SHOPPING LIST: Sherry, port, Madeira, Australian Liqueur Muscat.

The fab four: the world's most famous grape group

CABERNET SAUVIGNON

Cabernet Sauvignon carries the same well-travelled suitcase as Chardonnay (they are often seen sharing the same trolley). He boasts as many air-miles, is equally unfussy about what climate he ends up in, and – like his white partner – gets whisked through fast-track immigration simply by wafting his French (in this case, claret-coloured) documents.

You can't fail to spot Cabernet Sauvignon in a room full of his varietal friends. It's that aftershave he wears (blackcurrant and cassis, with a faint hint of mint), that same deep colour of his outfit and that strong, tannic grip of his handshake.

Alone, he's a bit of a boring old chap (it's okay; he can take it – he's thick-skinned), but get him together with his pals Merlot and Cabernet Franc, and he becomes far more entertaining. He can do the youthful, flirty thing, but to be honest, he prefers that serious, rather odd relationship that requires a long separation in a dark, damp place and a reunion where everyone applauds his new, softer, more complex character.

At his worst (cheap claret), he is a thin, bony individual with a herbaceous streak and aggressive tendencies. At his most charming (Chile), he is a ripe, fleshy, blind-taster's dream, and at his best (old claret), he is one of the most beguiling and complex characters you'll ever want to meet.

THE PACKAGE: Blackcurrants, cassis, cedar, pencil lead, chocolate, tannin, vanilla, meat, leather and capsicum.

THE LINGO: Complex, structure, backbone, serious, classic, ageing potential.

THE ASTON MARTINS: For the world's greatest Cabernet blends, you'll need to go to Bordeaux (the Left Bank and the money bank). For New World Classics, look to California (Napa), Washington State, Australia (Barossa, Margaret River, Eden Valley) and Chile (Maipo).

THE VOLVOS: Bulgaria, Chile and Southwest France all make Cabernets that regularly meet the necessary domestic-appliance standards.

CHARDONNAY

Quite simply, the world's favourite white wine (pronounced 'Shardnay' by the *Bridget Jones* generation) has become so popular that some drinkers mistakenly think it is a brand rather than a grape variety.

Chardonnay is the wine-drinker's flexible friend, offering the reliability of a Volvo with all the enjoyment of a soft-top MG. It is always there when you need it: when you can't understand the wine list, when you've been dumped (or want to celebrate dumping someone), when you need a funeral wine to comfort everyone or a wedding wine that won't offend the older or younger generations.

Yet if you stop and ask drinkers why they love Chardonnay so much, they'll scratch their heads and try (and usually fail) to pin down those nebulous flavours they love so much. Perhaps this is because Chardonnay is often more a feel than a flavour – no other grape produces a wine that can be immediately recognized by the way it sits on the tongue and rolls around the mouth. But while there is often a common thread, it is a fallacy to say this grape produces a homogeneous mass of wine styles.

From the crisp and steely Chablis to the rich, buttery mouthful of West Coast sunshine, Chardonnay wears a coat of many colours, aromas and flavours.

THE PACKAGE: Butter, nuts, toast and tropical fruit at one end to minerals, smoke, apple and citrus fruits at the other.

THE LINGO: Oaky, fat, rich, golden, 'citrussy', flinty, leesy, ripe.

THE ASTON MARTINS: Head to Burgundy (take a guide and a rich friend), California (take sunglasses and a chainsaw), and the cooler parts of Australia (take a map of Adelaide Hills) and New Zealand (take a break from Sauvignon Blanc).

THE VOLVOS: For something solid and reliable, look to Chile, Argentina, South Africa, the warmer bits of Australia, and the Languedoc region of France.

MERLOT

Safe, reliable and guaranteed not to cause any embarrassment when ordered off the wine list, Merlot is best described as red Chardonnay. Personally, I prefer to refer to it as the John Candy of the varietal family: a big-hearted, cuddly character whose ability to make people smile is far too often underrated.

Traditionally appearing as a support act to the main Cabernet event, Merlot has – thanks to an American adoration for red wine that's as easy to drink as white – taken to its solo role with relish. In the US in the mid-1990s, Merlot-mania took off to such an extent that some producers started shipping it in bulk from Chile just to keep up with demand, and this grape variety began appearing on interior designers' colour charts.

At its worst, it is as boring as Céline Dion, producing endless numbers of seemingly identical soft, slushy MOR hits that you've forgotten five minutes after drinking. At its best, it delivers one of the most hedonistic pleasures in the world: soft, velvety wines that offer the drinking equivalent of a long, lingering kiss under a warm duvet on a wet Sunday morning.

Best drunk young, it can nevertheless perform cartwheels (did someone mention Pomerol?) at Zimmer-frame age.

THE PACKAGE: Bright, crimson colours, juicy berry fruit, chocolate and cream.

THE LINGO: Lush, exotic, voluptuous, unctuous, supple, round, velvety, gluggable, moreish, sexy.

THE ASTIN MARTINS: France's Saint-Emilion and Pomerol make the most hedonistic and collectable Merlots in the world, with the New World chasing hard from California (Carneros and Alexander Valley), Washington State (Walla Walla), New Zealand (Hawke's Bay) and Chile (Cachapoal Valley).

THE VOLVOS: Chile makes the best quaffing material out of Merlot, and there are plenty of good, soft, ripe wines coming out of the south of France.

SAUVIGNON BLANC

If you had to attach grape varieties to famous personalities, Sauvignon Blanc would definitely be Sir Les Patterson. There's absolutely no mistaking the loud, extrovert, occasionally rude (cat's pee on a gooseberry bush and sweaty armpits) act, and opinion is split between those who love its in-yer-face appeal and those who find it unsubtle, aggressive and far too pungent.

With its distinctive aromas of gooseberry, grass and asparagus, Sauvignon Blanc is the greatest wake-up wine in the world (God must have created it over brunch) and one of the easiest wines to spot in blind tastings. Unlike its three friends, however, it doesn't perform well everywhere and only the cooler spots (like Marlborough in New Zealand, the Loire Valley in France, the Casablanca Valley in Chile) seem to get the best out if it.

The Kiwis can be thanked for lifting this grape onto the podium, and Sauvignon Blanc has returned the complement by putting New Zealand on the global wine map.

No other white wine has ever made such a startling debut or such a lasting impression as those first great gooseberry depth-charges from Marlborough. There are some – the Americans in particular – who think this grape works well with oak, but for me, the best versions are the ones made from 100 percent unadulterated fruit. If you really want to make your mouth water, Sauvignon Blanc is the grape to do the job.

THE PACKAGE: Cut grass, gooseberries, asparagus, passion-fruit, tinned peas, cat's pee and citrus fruits.

THE LINGO: Pungent, leafy, fresh, zingy, flinty, refreshing, sharp.

THE ASTIN MARTINS: For something tangy and green, look to the Loire (Sancerre and Pouilly Fumé), and if you want the aromatic speakers set at 11, New Zealand (Marlborough) should help wake you up.

THE VOLVOS: Bordeaux makes crisp, refreshing whites, but my tips for excellent-value Sauvignon are Chile (particularly Casablanca) and Hungary.

The magnificent seven: a posse of boredom-beating classics

Syrah

Dark as the bruises on a cowboy's bum, Syrah (or Shiraz, as the Aussies call it) is the hot red grape of the moment. If Tom Jones wanted to serve a wine that would provoke as much knicker-throwing as his *Delilah* performance, this is the grape to choose.

WHAT YOU GET: Inky-black colour, pepper, blackberries, earth, smoke, chocolate.

WHERE TO HEAD: The Rhône Valley and all around Australia.

STYLES: Black and broody in the Rhône, big-boned and spicy in Australia's Barossa.

Pinot Noir

This is the thinking-person's grape, the arthouse production with subtitles and a complex plot, the Holy Grail, the life-affirming experience, the thing that makes you realize a wine can change your life. It is also a fickle little performer, a magnet for wine geeks, and a cause of far too many nerdy wine conversations.

WHAT YOU GET: Pale colours, soft (mainly red) berry fruits, silky texture.

WHERE TO HEAD: Burgundy, New Zealand, Oregon and cool parts of Australia.

STYLES: Seductive and sexy in Burgundy, flirtatious and funky in the New World.

Sémillon/Semillon

If the big man upstairs had forgotten to invent Chardonnay, the little guys downstairs would now be making tankerloads of Sémillon. The fruit is more citrus-fruit than tropical, it has a good, full texture, and if you've got patience, it has the potential to age spectacularly. In Bordeaux, it normally ends up partnering Sauvignon Blanc, but Australia is where it really shines.

WHAT YOU GET: Lemon, toast, bacon, smoke, lanolin, honey.

WHERE TO HEAD: Australia's Hunter Valley and Bordeaux.

STYLES: Luscious sweet wines (Sauternes), crisp, blended whites (Bordeaux) and beguiling oldies (Australia).

Riesling

The one in the tall, brown bottles, the one the critics adore, the one that's harder to sell than a fake BMW, the one that matches food better than any other white wine, and the one that can be piercingly dry and tooth-rattlingly sweet.

Forget fashion, forget Liebfraumilch; remember Riesling.

WHAT YOU GET: Lime, lemon, honey, minerals, kerosene, petrol.

WHERE TO HEAD: Germany, Australia (Clare Valley), France (Alsace).

STYLES: Citrus fruit in Australia, minerals and petrol in Germany, spices in Alsace.

Zinfandel

The big Zin is California's very own trump-card grape (okay, they might have nicked it from southern Italy, but let's not argue), and boy, have they squeezed the maximum out of it. Pink 'blush' wines; simple, juicy reds; intense, sturdy blockbusters: name a style and you can bet there's a Zinfandel model for it. The best are deep-coloured, rich, concentrated, full-bodied and high in alcohol.

WHAT YOU GET: Blackberries, plums, spice, tannin.

WHERE TO HEAD: California (Sierra Foothills, Mendocino County, Napa, Sonoma).

STYLES: Everything from rosé to broody blockbusters.

Sangiovese

The name behind a million raffia-covered Chianti bottles, Sangiovese can be both depressingly mediocre and breathtakingly brilliant in the space of a price-jump on a wine list. When it's given plenty of TLC, it tastes and feels as sexy as it sounds. When it's taken seriously, it ends up being one of the most beautiful, bitter-sweet drinking experiences there is.

WHAT YOU GET: Cherries, plums, dried fruits, bitter almonds.

WHERE TO HEAD: Tuscany.

STYLES: Basic quaffing Chianti to mega-priced cult wines.

Viognier

The gentlest, most soothing form of aromatherapy you can get. Stick your nose above a glass of Viognier and in seconds the flames of stress have been wafted out by rich, heady scents of apricot, honey and flowers. In the mouth, it feels rich and seductive, and despite being dry, there is a teasing sweetness in its core.

WHAT YOU GET: Viagra and Prozac rolled into one.

WHERE TO HEAD: Northern Rhône.

STYLES: Mind-blowing (Condrieu) to mind-settling (south of France, California, Australia).

The dirty dozen: 12 ugly-duckling grapes that make beautiful wines

Albariño (white)

The grape behind Spain's most expensive white wines delivers beautiful, peach-scented whites that lift ordinary paella to gastronomic heights. Drink them young.

WHAT YOU GET: Peaches, apricots, refreshing acidity.

WHERE TO HEAD: Galicia in northwest Spain.

Assyrtico (white)

'Ass-what?' I hear you all say. No, I haven't lost my Elgin marbles: this is one of the great white-wine grapes of the world. It delivers bone-dry, crisp, piercingly intense wines in a climate that could bake the hind legs off a tourist-carrying donkey.

WHAT YOU GET: Pale colours, minerals, steely acidity.

WHERE TO HEAD: Santorini and other Aegean islands.

Carmenère (red)

An old Bordeaux variety now living a far happier life in Chile. For a long time it was confused with Merlot, but thanks to better press, Carmenère is now poised for stardom.

WHAT YOU GET: Plums, chocolate, spice.

WHERE TO HEAD: Chile.

Chenin Blanc (white)

From simple, apple-edged quaffing wine to jaw-dropping displays of sweet, luscious, liquid pyrotechnics, Chenin has more tricks up its sleeve than David Copperfield. The dessert wines can last for decades.

WHAT YOU GET: Apple, quince, honey, wet straw, waxy textures.

WHERE TO HEAD: The Loire Valley (serious) and South Africa (fun).

Gamay (red)

There is no way you'll get me to admit that I like this bubblegum-scented red, but give me a chilled glass of Beaujolais in summer and I guarantee I'll be humming with content in seconds. Drink it young (but not *nouveau*).

WHAT YOU GET: Strawberries, raspberries.

WHERE TO HEAD: Beaujolais.

Malbec (red)

Malbec was forced into exile and ended up living a new life in South America. It changed its face and clothes so much that it now bears little resemblance to the photo in its French passport.

WHAT YOU GET: Blackberries, earth, chocolate, minerals.

WHERE TO HEAD: Argentina and Southwest France (Cahors).

Muscat (white)

The only wine that smells of grapes. In summer, it offers dry, fragrant, spicy assistance, while in winter it can provide mood-soothing, sweet, hedonistic flavour.

WHAT YOU GET: Grapes, raisins, orange peel, roses, honey.

WHERE TO HEAD: South of France, Australia.

Nebbiolo (red)

If you feel your tongue has become a bit too relaxed with all the soft wines around – a tannic workout with Nebbiolo is due. Often brutish, always beguiling, best in the company of a large winter stew.

WHAT YOU GET: Tar, roses, meat, tobacco, sweet-and-sour.

WHERE TO HEAD: Piedmont, Italy.

Pinotage (red)

You get both beauty and the beast with Pinotage. But whether you love it or hate it, there is no denying that this grape has bags of personality.

WHAT YOU GET: Damsons, plums, bananas.

WHERE TO HEAD: South Africa.

Pinot Gris (white)

When dressed up in Italian togs (Pinot Grigio), this member of the Pinot family delivers crisp, floral-scented white wines. In Alsace, it slips into a far richer costume and performs a more serious routine.

WHAT YOU GET: Honey, smoke, floral aromas, spice, apple, lemon.

WHERE TO HEAD: Northern Italy, Alsace, Oregon, Hungary.

Touriga Nacional (red)

If the British hadn't invented port, Douro table wines might be as highly revered as claret, and Touriga Nacional (the region's muscular lead player) could be enjoying as much respect as Cabernet Sauvignon. Honest.

WHAT YOU GET: Dark colours, black-fruit flavours, chunky tannins.

WHERE TO HEAD: Portugal.

Verdelho (white)

Performs better in table-wine attire than in its fortified guise. Having travelled to the other side of the world from its home in Madeira, Verdelho is enjoying a second life as a citric white wine with an unmistakable Aussie personality.

WHAT YOU GET: Lime, lemon.

WHERE TO HEAD: Australia.

The four worlds of wine

Most of us are used to dividing the world into two neat halves. On one side we have the Old World, where tradition, *terroir* and indecipherable front labels abound. On the other we have the New World, where technology, brands and clichéd back labels are the norm.

It wasn't that long ago that the phrase 'New World' was used patronizingly to describe some foul-tasting concoction that someone had brought back on a trip to the southern hemisphere. But then the Californians and Australians came along and changed everything, and in the blink of a couple of decent vintages, being New World suddenly became a very positive USP (unique selling point) indeed.

Not only did it refer to a particular style of wine, it also inferred an attitude and a state of mind. To be a New World winemaker was to be experimental, dynamic and exciting. To be an Old World *vigneron* was to be stuck in the mud (sorry, *terroir*) and boring. New World wines meant accessible flavours and soft textures, while Old World equalled complexity and a generous coating of tannin.

Today, however, this simple divide no longer exists. Ideas have been stolen, principles copied, techniques borrowed and raw materials swapped. Today, the two worlds have become so mixed up and intertwined that putting the tags 'New World' or 'Old World' in front of a wine tells you virtually nothing about the style of drink you can expect.

The Old World that likes being Old

To these guys, the word 'brand' is still a swear word, and putting the grape variety on the label is a cardinal sin. They do what they do because it worked for their fathers, so why shouldn't it work for them? They don't believe there is such a thing as a winemaker (well, except when an award has to be picked up) and wine is something that is created in the vineyard, not the winery.

CLASSIC EXAMPLE: An old-style Barolo that requires a 20-year cellar sentence to reform its character.

The Old World that wants to be New

This group has taken one look at the New World sales graph and decided, 'Yes, please, we'll have a piece of that, too.' They've changed their vineyards to get riper fruit and sunnier flavours, they've invested in new wineries to help get those flavours in the bottle, they've opened their doors to foreign consultants, and they've introduced new, consumer-friendly packaging.

CLASSIC EXAMPLE: A modern brand from the Languedoc that tastes like it could have come from anywhere.

The New World that's proud to be New

This group of winemakers still dominates the New World. They believe firmly in the principle of making a wine that ordinary drinkers (rather than wine snobs and critics) want, and they are not afraid to use whatever technological innovation is necessary to achieve that goal. 'Anything goes' is their motto, winemakers are their idols, and fruit is their Holy Grail. They believe in brands, varietal labelling, synthetic corks, blends and value for money.

CLASSIC EXAMPLE: An Australian Chardonnay/Sauvignon Blanc blend using machine-picked fruit from two different regions, special fast-fermenting yeast and a muslin bag full of oak chips.

The New World that wishes it were Old

A small but growing minority of producers in the New World has decided that to be taken seriously requires a little Old World behaviour. This bunch is setting up appellations, easing up on human intervention, letting the climate take more control, talking about dirt with passion, taking the grape variety off the label, and charging Old World prices. These are the producers who want their wines to have a sense of place rather than a sense of fun, they want a waiting list for their mailing list, they want respect... and they want it all now.

CLASSIC EXAMPLE: A new premium, two-syllable-name wine made using fruit from a special patch of old vines, wild yeast, new French *barriques* and a very heavy bottle.

Wine joins the brand pack

Brands: wines with a sense of anywhere-ness

It's hard to remember the first wine we ever drank – probably because it was only a sip, and most vicars don't like revealing their sources – but most of us should be able to put a name to the first bottle of wine we ever bought.

Mine was Ernest & Julio Gallo's White Zinfandel, and I distinctly recall that the purchase of this slightly sweet California confection was seen (by me, at least) to be an upward move on the ladder of sophistication. There were no embarrassed giggles, no one turned the same blush colour as the wine, and the experience made me want to drink more (not less) of this fermented grape-juice stuff. Bottom line: I enjoyed it.

Almost all of us start our journey into wine appreciation at the friendly service station called Branded Wines. Faced with a complex subject that combines foreign languages, geography, social history, agricultural studies and acute sensory evaluation (ie, being able to taste), it's hardly surprising that most of us panic and head towards something that is recognizable, understandable and safe.

Brands help us step out of the lager lake and onto the first rung of the wine ladder. Brands are easy to find, easy to choose and easy to drink. And whatever else you might think of them, you can't help but admit that a lot of skill goes into creating them. Compared with the task of trying to make 30 million litres of Jacob's Creek every year (and keep the flavours constant no matter what the vintage throws at you), producing a few barrels of Château Lafite is an absolute doddle.

Today, however, there are growing fears that brands are becoming too widespread and powerful. The wine world might not yet have its equivalent of a Coke or a Budweiser, but with giant beer companies such as Fosters moving into wine, the chance of it being fermented under licence in different countries is increasing fast. Would you think twice about drinking Lindemans Bin 65 if it had 'Made in France' in small print on the bottom of the label?

Somehow, I doubt it. Most brands don't taste of a particular place – they have a sense of anywhere-ness rather than somewhere-ness – so it shouldn't and wouldn't make much difference if a particular brand were made all over the world.

My own personal gripe is that wine brands – like boy bands and washing powders – are all becoming worryingly similar, and this sea of similarity is threatening to submerge the small, independent producers who make wine the challenging quest that it is.

Most supermarket aisles are now dominated by big names, and if we allow this situation to reach full saturation point, essentially we'll be turning our backs on the world of the site-specific, the vintage-variable, the small-scale and the idiosyncratic. If that happens, the soul of wine will have disappeared, and the only letters you'll see branded on wine labels will be 'RIP'.

The good things about brands
- They're reliable: despite the fickleness of nature, most brands – thanks to winemaking technology and blending – are pretty much the same year on year.
- They're cheap: they allow you to afford to drink wine regularly.
- They're value for money: you (usually) get a drinkable wine at a good price.
- They're pronounceable: you don't have to master languages to order one.
- They're widely available: you can find them everywhere.

The bad things about brands
- They're boring: they all seem to taste the same.
- They're geographically ambiguous: they all taste like they could have come from anywhere.
- They're man-made: to make a wine the same every year requires a lot of intervention and manipulation.
- They're not very fashionable: most people don't want to be seen drinking something that everyone else is drinking.
- They're often too sweet: a spoonful of residual sugar helps the wine go down.

Life beyond brands: wines with roots

I don't remember much about my university days (the result of a very cheap student bar), but one lecture I do remember was about this thing called environmental determinism. No, don't turn over the page; bear with me on this.

The gist of it was as follows. The behaviour of all human beings is affected by the environment in which they live, so if you come from a hot, sunny place, you'll work, rest and play in a totally different way to someone who comes from a cold, dark place. If you took, say, a Norwegian and a Jamaican and asked them to do the same thing for a day (in a neutral climate), the theory of environmental determinism would lead you to predict that they'd act in very different ways. Their actions would be conditioned by the places from which they came.

So what has all this got to do with wine? Well, wines suffer (or rather benefit) from environmental determinism, too. Like people, wines have origins and, like people, they have a sense of somewhere-ness in their characters and

personalities. A German Riesling is a nervy, tightly strung wine because it comes from a place where it is a struggle to make wine. A Chilean Merlot, on the other hand, tastes soft, ripe and happy because it comes from a place that is basically a holiday camp for grapes. And a New Zealand Sauvignon Blanc is clean, green, and 100 percent pure fruit because the vines grow in a country that is – well, you've seen the tourism posters.

The French have developed a word for this sense of identity and it is *terroir*.

Terroir is the sum of all the environmental factors that affect a vine and therefore the wine that is produced from it. Each vineyard will have a particular soil, a particular slope and a particular climate, and all these will influence the character of the grapes and the juice squeezed from them. So, in theory, you should be able to guess where a wine comes from simply by tasting it and spotting the imprint left by its surroundings. Every wine should have its very own environmental DNA.

To a lot of people, *terroir* is the cornerstone on which a love of wine is built. To others, it is an overused marketing device responsible for making wine far more expensive than it needs to be. But even if you side with the anti-*terroir* camp, it's hard not to agree with the general philosophy behind the word.

Unless you are someone who likes your wines to taste the same no matter where they come from or what vintage they are made in, you can't fail to embrace the idea that wine is as chaotic and challenging as a United Nations' conference without translators. There are thousands upon thousands of wines, each with its own specific identity, each speaking a different language and each carrying its own snapshot of where it came from and what happened to it over the course of one year.

Dive into this world, and you can become a global explorer, a geological prospector and a meteorologist all in one. What's more, you can do this with just a corkscrew and a glass and conduct your investigations without ever having to travel further than your nearest bottle shop.

There is a catch, of course. Unlike the world of brands – where catchy names on labels are the only signposts you need to follow – the directions in *terroir*-land are a lot harder to read. Appellation names (it'll say 'AC Thingamajig' on a French label) and regions (the New World alternative) are your basic routefinders; then there are specific vineyards to discover and vintages to follow.

Sometimes you'll find yourself going round in circles, and there are bound to be some unpleasant experiences (there is bad *terroir* as well as good *terroir*) that make you wonder why you didn't stay put in Jacob's Creek. But once you begin to match flavours to places, and when the day comes that you do a blind tasting and manage to put a place to a bottle without looking at the label, then you'll realize just how extraordinary this drink is and why you can never go back to brands.

Organic wines

Organic wine has never been more popular. Once deemed overpriced, unreliable and about as fashionable as yoga, it is suddenly as sexy as, well, yoga. Thanks to the public awareness generated by various food scares and the genetic-modification debate, drinkers have at last begun to scrutinize their drinks as closely as their food. You won't find 'Made from grapes grown with the use of chemical fertilizers, pesticides and fungicides' on a back label, but you need only visit a few large commercial vineyards to see that they have been (and still are) widely used. Armed with this knowledge and a growing concern for the environment, wine-drinkers are now putting their weight behind the organic movement.

Not surprisingly, winemakers and importers have rushed to join the green bandwagon, leaving the organic picture looking increasingly fuzzy around the edges. Besides the fact that levels of organic-ness come in various shades of grey, and organic standards (and policing) vary widely from country to country, there is also a lack of clarity about organic certification. Just to confuse matters further, some wine producers are making organic wines but aren't mentioning the fact on their labels. To say it's a bit of an organic jungle out there is an understatement.

What is organic wine?
Definitions vary. According to European laws, there is still no such thing as an organic wine, only 'wine made from organic grapes'. By that they mean grapes grown without the use of synthetic fertilizers, pesticides, insecticides, weed-killers or other chemical sprays. In theory, an organic wine should also have a minimal amount of chemical intervention in the winery, and sulphur levels – one of the few permitted chemical additives – should be low or (under some countries' regulations) zero.

Are organic wines more expensive, and if so, why?
You may have to pay marginally more for organic wine, but this is due largely to the increased costs of labour-intensive organic viticulture. Hence you don't find many cheap organic brands on the shelves.

What wines will you miss out on if you stick to organic wines?
Although you can buy organic wines

from most parts of the world, some climates are more suitable than others, and some countries are more active in the organic movement than others. For example, there are lots of organic French wines but not many Australian or Chilean versions. Also, most of the world's so-called blue-chip wines are not organic.

Do organic wines taste different from non-organic wines?

Organic wine production is cleaner in its principles, but that doesn't necessarily mean the end product will taste cleaner. If there is a taste difference between organic and non-organic, it is that the former tends to be a purer expression of site and vintage. Intensity of flavour might not be different, but fluctuations in flavour may be noticeable.

Is it true you don't get a hangover if you drink organic wine?

Unfortunately, evidence is only anecdotal, but there does seem support (certainly in the wine-writing fraternity) that the lower levels of sulphur in organic wines help reduce the chances of a headache the morning after. Then again, if you overindulge it makes no difference.

Do organic wines make you feel better?

If by feeling better you mean having a clean conscience about what you've just bought and knowing that you've made a positive contribution to a cleaner earth, then the answer has to be yes.

What is biodynamics all about?

Biodynamic viticulture is an extreme form of organic grape-growing. It involves working in harmony with planetary forces (moon cycles are very important) and having a wider view of environmental forces and balance. Despite the level of commitment required, biodynamism is being taken up by a growing number of winemakers.

What is a vegetarian-friendly wine?

These are wines that have not used animal-based products (like gelatin and isinglass) to clean, or 'fine', the wine. For it to be suitable for vegans as well, the wine should not have been fined with egg whites.

Cult wines

In 1984, an Australian winemaker called David Hohnen flew to New Zealand with a mission to make a premium New World white wine that people would sit up and notice. He found himself a winemaker, built a winery in Marlborough, designed a label that would be instantly recognized across any crowded restaurant in any part of the world and came up with a name that no one could forget.

The wine was, of course, Cloudy Bay, and thanks to a combination of shrewd marketing and good old word of mouth, it soon became as much a dinner-table fashion accessory as a fine example of Kiwi Sauvignon Blanc. Even today – when the label is under corporate rather than cult ownership – you only need to hear the words 'It's here' or 'I've managed to get you one' and you immediately know which wine is being talked about.

Meanwhile, a few years before Hohnen went in search of gooseberry-scented gold, a Belgian called Jacques Thienpont went to France, bought himself a small patch of Pomerol soil and began making minute quantities of red wine. Unlike his Antipodean counterpart, Thienpont never had a marketing plan or a sexy image, but a combination of rarity (only a few hundred cases were produced), *terroir* (just up the road from Château Pétrus) and critical approval helped Le Pin become the biggest cult wine of them all. Even with the market deflation caused by the Asian slump, you'd still have to hand over £15,000 if you wanted to buy a case of the 1982 vintage today.

In their own particular ways, both Le Pin and Cloudy Bay have had a profound impact on the image and perception of wine. More than ever before, rich consumers see wine as another collectable that can help reduce their bank balances, while would-be wine producers see it as a means of increasing their bank balances. From the path that these two wines have forged, a cult-wine phenomenon has emerged.

Compared with films (where you might get a couple of hits a year), the wine industry has been pumping out new cult material at a prolific rate. Some have productions that are so small it's hard to find anyone who has actually seen a bottle, let alone drunk one. Others have generated such strong demand that they have to set up waiting lists for the main mailing lists. One Australian cult producer recently decided that, because so many people wanted his wine, it was fairest (and best for PR purposes) if he sold it to the highest bidders on his website. It brings a whole new meaning to the expression 'having the right connections'.

So how does a wine attain cult status? Size is obviously a crucial element, because rarity has enormous cachet in collecting circles. So you buy yourself a nice little patch of vines – preferably red grapes, because red wine is more fashionable than white these days – and quietly you begin making small quantities (definitely fewer than 1,000 cases) of a wine produced to a specific critic-pleasing formula. In particular it must be pleasing to a certain Robert Parker, Jr, whose 100-point

scoring system is followed religiously by wealthy wine-drinkers everywhere. The taste descriptors you're looking for are 'rich', 'opulent', 'concentrated', 'smooth', 'creamy' and 'ripe', and the score you need is 95 and over.

There are a few other elements that can generate extra cult points. A daft name (like Duck Muck Shiraz or Pingus) is a good idea, as is an eccentric winemaker, an ironic winery statement (a shed instead of a château) and an allocation policy that spreads the wine out in such minute parcels that securing a bottle requires extraordinary amounts of perseverance. Do all these things and top it all off with a pricing policy that involves thinking of a number between one and 20, adding your age to that number and then doubling it, and you are ready to become the new Tarantino of the wine world.

There is just one problem. At the moment, so many cult wines are out there that cultdom itself is in danger of going out of fashion. And if that happens, trophy-wine prices will shrink as fast as they grew.

GREATEST PUNCHING FIGHT IN RING HISTORY

MAD.SQ.GARDEN

10 ROUNDS 'SPARKLING' 10 ROUNDS

WINE
VS.
'FIZZ'
CHAMPAGNE

OTHER GREAT BOUTS

Fizzy wines vs champers

CHAMPAGNE

The British might have been putting bubbles into wine before the French, but it is the latter, of course, who have turned fizzy wine into one of the most successful commercial ventures in the world.

Almost every wedding couple gets toasted on it, every sporting victor gets doused in it, every boat gets launched with it, and every business deal gets sealed with it. More than any other type of wine, Champagne is about feeling good (it's not a great funeral favourite). It is about status and brand loyalty ('I only drink Cristal, darling'), and about drinking rather than analysing.

Compared with the scrutiny given to claret and burgundy, you'll find far fewer tasting notes scribbled about Champagne. There might be a brief recognition of how dry and acidic it is and how fine the beads of bubbles are, but there is rarely great deliberation over the minutiae of flavour. Ask what people love about it and most (of the honest ones) will say something like, 'It makes my tongue tingle, my head giddy, and my mood extremely positive'.

But is there really such a big difference between one brand and another, and between the cheap stuff and the mega-priced super cuvées? The answer is yes and no. At the bottom end of the market, I personally find it hard to distinguish one bottle of green, raw acidity from another; they all trigger the same Mr Bean-style facial expressions and they all taste better with a dash of cassis.

At the other end of the scale, the investment does pay off. Acidity is gentler and more rounded, flavours are richer and nuttier, and bubbles are finer and longer-lasting. Instead of a ham-fisted, frothy massage, a top Champagne feels more like delicate oral acupuncture.

BUYING ADVICE: Good sparkling wine tastes far nicer than cheap Champagne. One bottle of decent vintage Champagne is better than two nasty non-vintages, and special cuvées are a waste of money.

SPARKLING WINE

The sparkling-wine brigade has the massive hurdle of trying to persuade you to look past the inferiority complex attached to their wines' names. No matter how you say it or in what accent you pronounce it, sparkling wine just doesn't sound as good as the classy 'sshhh' of Champagne. And that's exactly how the men of Reims and Epernay like it. You can use their equipment, copy their methods (even steal some of their staff), but if your little CO_2 experiment didn't take place in Champagne, you cannot legally call it Champagne.

Sparkling wine varies enormously in quality and price. The cheapest bulk productions offer something that tastes and feels like wine shoved through a Sodastream machine. The best – those that attempt to replicate the raw materials and techniques found in northeast France – can fool even the most determined of experts in blind tastings.

As with property values, the most important thing is location, location, location. If you can find places where the grapes really have to struggle to ripen and where ripeness comes with bracing acidity attached, you might just stand a chance of achieving the elegance, power and sharp-edged structure found in the Bollys, Veuves and Dom Pérignons of this world.

Today, the highest-quality sparkling wines come from the cooler regions of Australia (Tasmania and Yarra Valley), New Zealand, California, and – no, this isn't a typo – England. With its chalk soils and long growing season, the latter has probably the greatest chance of beating the Champenois at their own game. It may take another couple of decades of trial and error, investment and global warming, but the chances of a Champagne house hopping across the Channel to make sparkling wine are increasing every vintage.

BUYING ADVICE: Sparkling wines made by Champagne companies (Mumm, Domaine Chandon, Roederer), sparkling red wines from Australia, Crémant de Loire, English sparkling wine (Nyetimber, South Ridge).

Dessert wines: *la dolce vita*

STICKIES

Sometimes our eating and drinking habits make no sense. Here we are, all happily stuffing ourselves with sugar-filled goodies all day long, yet when someone suggests a liquid version we either look embarrassed at the suggestion or tap our tummies and say, 'I'd better not.'

If dessert came at the start rather than the end of the meal, and if old people preferred drinking dry material rather than sweet, then maybe things would be different. Sweet wines – or 'stickies', as the Aussies call them – would be the hippest sip on the block. You'd be able to talk noble rot and everyone would know what you were on about.

By steering clear of the sweet end of the wine spectrum you are missing out on some of the most divine flavours and hedonistic textures ever created. These are wines that dribble rather than drip, glide rather than pour, and settle on the tongue rather than slosh around the mouth. These are wines to be sipped and savoured like medicinal treats and – with a bit of imagination – they can hit the sort of sensory buttons you probably thought only Viagra could reach.

Finally, for those of you who avoid sweet wine for fear of adding inches to your waistline, it's worth remembering that most of the calories in wine come from the alcohol, not the sugar. A glass of sweet wine has about 125 calories, a glass of Champagne has about 95, and a single portion of Christmas pudding has nearly 300. So there you go: it's not such a dietary crime after all.

Late-picked grapes

The simplest method of making sweet wines is to leave the grapes on the vines a bit longer than normal and pick them when their sugar levels are higher. In New World countries such as Australia, these are called late-harvest wines; they tend to be the simplest, lightest and most affordable members of the sticky fraternity. In Germany, things get more complicated, because there can be a whole family of late-harvest wines (ranked from *Auslese* to *Trockenbeerenauslese*), each with a higher level of sweetness and price.

Mouldy grapes

The sight of a bunch of shrivelled, mould-speckled grapes might not seem a good cause for excitement, but if you make sweet wines, it is enough to make you want to kiss your bank manager. *Botrytis cinerea*, or noble rot, is an airborne fungus that attaches itself to the grapes and, like a parasite, dehydrates them until all that is left is a disgusting-looking carcass. But squeeze this ugly clump and out comes an intense, concentrated juice with a particular *botrytis*-affected flavour. The most famous rot-blessed wine is Sauternes, and from personal experience, I'd say it's one of the best mood-improving drugs that money can buy.

Sun-dried grapes

In some parts of the world, grapes are picked and then left on racks (or on mats outside) to dry until they look more like raisins than grapes. These are then squeezed and the now-concentrated juice is fermented into a deliciously rich dessert wine. Famous examples of this style include Samos Muscat from Greece, *vin de paille* from the Jura in France and *vin santo* from Italy.

Frozen grapes

Another way of getting extra sweetness and concentration is to allow the grapes to freeze on the vine. These are then crushed as normal, and the difference in freezing points between water and sugar solution allows the sweet juice to be separated from the ice. In Germany, this style of sweet wine is known as *Eiswein* (ice wine in other parts of the world) and such are the risks and tiny volumes associated with it, prices are far from frozen.

Don't be afraid to ditch the glass

Some sweet wines have such high levels of concentration and viscosity – such as Hungary's nectar-like Tokáji Eszencia – that they are almost too thick to drink. When the going gets too sticky, don't be afraid to change their job descriptions from drink to food. Pour them over ice-cream, soak fruit in them or just take them to bed and have some fun. (A partner would help with the last suggestion.)

Club 18 to 25 (ABV): no smoking jacket required

If I told you that sherry is one of the sexiest wines on the shelves, you'd probably think I was a few drops short of a full *copita*. And guess what? You'd be wrong.

If I suggested that Madeira was the most underrated, underpriced and underappreciated wine in the world, you'd probably conclude that I had recently invested in a small patch of the eponymous volcanic island it comes from. And again, you'd be way off the mark.

Finally, if I tried to persuade you that port could be drunk without a pair of slippers, a smoking jacket and a dose of acute embarrassment, well, you'd probably wonder whether the research for this book had finally taken its toll on the grey stuff. A good guess, but sorry, booze hasn't taken its toll just yet.

To all those who are still with me (and you can't all be vicars, grannies and retired army generals), let me welcome you to Club Fortified. It may look a little stuffy from the outside, but once through the door and away from your sniggering friends, you'll find yourself having a better time than you expected – and I'm certain you'll back up what I've just said about the so-called 'oldies' favourites'.

As the name suggests, fortified wines are wines that have been given a strengthening boost of alcohol. Yet depending on the type of base wine you start with and the exact moment that you apply the boost, you can end up with different styles and flavours. In the end, higher alcohol levels are just about the only common thread linking this motley crew.

Tangy appetite-builders

Just as some people believe fortified wine is drunk only in retirement homes and gentlemen's clubs, it is also a misconception that all fortified wines are sweet. Most sherry is dry, and when served chilled it performs one of the most refreshingly different pre-meal routines since your grandmother did her pretzel-juggling trick. Fino is a pale-coloured sherry with a characteristic tangy, yeast-fuelled bite. Manzanilla and Puerto Fino – both from areas nearer the coast of southern Spain – tend to be more delicate and saltier in character. All three go brilliantly with *tapas* and have alcohol levels that are no greater than your average bottle of Australian Shiraz. For something darker, nuttier and more full-bodied (but still dry), look for amontillados and olorosos.

In the Madeira fold, the Sercial grape produces a wonderfully dry, acidic style of wine. Last in these ranks are the dry styles of white port from Portugal.

Liquid comfort blankets

Some fortified wines are renowned for their silky textures and sweet, more-ish flavours. The leader of this soothing pack is Australian Liqueur Muscat. The best ones come from Rutherglen in Victoria, where a combination of super-ripe, highly aromatic Muscat grapes, spirit and long maturation in barrels creates a mahogany-coloured, toffee-tasting, viscous treat. Look out also for Liqueur Tokay, made from Muscadelle grapes. Other fortified wines that can be used either with desserts or as comforting solo material are oloroso *dulce* and the ultra-sweet Pedro Ximénez sherries,

the raisiny Mavrodaphne of Patras from Greece, and the Muscat-based *vin doux naturel* from France.

Cheese, cigars and long conversations

The third category of fortified wines are those that are traditionally drunk after a meal, when you want something warming and rich (but not too sweet) to take you into the wind-down zone. Port – the drink you pass to your left – is the obvious call, and the style you go for depends on a) whether you want to muck around with a decanter, and b) whether your bank balance has a light or heavy crust. If you don't want to decant, try an aged tawny (preferably at least a 20-year-old) or a late-bottled vintage (also known as an LBV). If you do like a bit of sediment separation and you do have cash to spare, a vintage port or its single-estate cousin, the single-quinta port, will provide something darker and more complex. You might also want to try one of the sweeter styles of Madeira. If you want the perfect antidote to clubbing, a glass of old Malmsey and a comfortable sofa is as good a remedy as you'll find.

Pre-dinner rumbles, post-dinner grumbles

PRE-DINNER DRINKS

In these days of fast food and on-the-hoof grazing, the pre-meal warm-up has become a bit of a forgotten social routine – which means the aperitif is about as fashionable as the hostess trolley. But just as you need to warm up before stepping into the sporting arena, so you should also limber up the stomach before putting it through its paces, and the aperitif (the word comes from the Latin *aperire*, 'to open') does exactly that. A glass of something cold, dry and sharp helps get the gastric juices flowing, the appetite stimulated, and the tummy rumbling in readiness for refuelling.

Every country has its own particular style of warm-up juice, and any one of the following will have you salivating like a Russian cosmonaut returning to earth after two months of space-station grub.

MANZANILLA An ice-cold glass of this tangy, salty style of sherry always gets the Pavlovian dinner bell going.

BRUT As in the dry style of Champagne, not the aftershave.

KIR This partnership of cassis and dry white wine is a great retro-aperitif. There is always the Kir Royal option, made with Champagne instead of wine, for that extra touch of sophistication.

CHILLED WHITE PORT Drier and lighter than the deep-red stuff, this is a Douro Valley favourite in summer.

VERMOUTH A herbally enhanced, fortified drink with a nice bitter kick.

PISCO SOURS Citrus-fruit-based cocktails can make great aperitifs, and Chile's gift to the global bar is a real wake-up call for the senses.

DRY GERMAN RIESLING Low in alcohol, crisp and flinty, there is nothing like a bit of liquid Vorsprung durch Technik to lubricate the jaw joints.

SAUTERNES A favourite French aperitif, but the kitchen is going to have to produce something pretty special to compete with this.

ROSÉ Go for the dry, crisp, Old World variety rather than the big and fruity New World ones.

FRUIT BEERS A glass of cherry *kriek* or raspberry *frambozen* is guaranteed to build an instant appetite.

POST-DINNER DRINKS

So the meal finishes. After the signal has been given, the gentlemen slip into their smoking jackets and, with a cigar in one hand and a glass the size of a goldfish bowl in the other, retire to a female-free zone to practise for the upcoming 'boring conversation' championships. Well, (hopefully) that's not how it happens today; if it does, you know it's time you got a new social life.

However, there's no need to throw a tantrum if someone offers you a Cognac or a digestif: these drinks might be associated with bizarre behaviour, but it isn't a terminal relationship. The end of the meal is the time to inhale aromas lazily rather than taking a quick sniff, to sip slowly rather than gulp greedily, to savour flavour rather than quench thirst. It is also a time for handing over the car keys to someone else.

GRAPPA Italy's little throat-warmer is having a bit of a renaissance. Look for the ones made from single grape varieties.

PORT For those who find the weight and social graces of vintage port (all that passing to the left malarkey) a bit too hard to handle, an aged tawny is a delicious alternative.

MADEIRA Probably the most underappreciated wine in the world. As soothing drinks go, it beats everything in this list by a mile.

SWEET SHERRIES Yes, sherry feels just as at home at 11PM as it does at 7PM. One sip of a dark, nutty oloroso *dulce*, and you'll be a convert for life.

COGNAC Don't drink it out of a balloon-shaped glass; you'll look like an idiot and all you will smell is alcohol.

ARMAGNAC The thinking-person's Cognac (so I'm told) but don't think, just drink.

TEQUILA The adventurous after-dinner sipper will pour a glass of *añejo-* (aged) style Tequila and savour rather than slam.

CALVADOS This apple distillate from Normandy is one of the most refreshing brandies in the world.

SINGLE-MALT WHISKIES There's nothing like the smell of peat, iodine and salty air to round off a good night.

BARLEY WINE If you want to finish the night on a beery note, this deep-coloured, malty ale makes a surprisingly good nightcap.

Food wines: matchmaking heaven or trainspotter hell

Picture this. You're in the supermarket wine aisle staring at a technicolour sea of labels, wondering what lifebuoy you should cling to before you sink into a state of hypnosis. You've got a budget to work to, you know what grape variety you like and you've located a style of wine that fits your mood. A decision is within reach.

With a relieved look on your face, you reach up to grab a bottle you recognize – but just as you make contact, the food-and-wine-matching monster appears. In a deep voice, it inquires innocently, 'Are you *sure* that'll go with the bung-in-the-oven fusion meal for one?' In a panic, you drop the bottle and run off to the sanctuary of the lager section.

Wine date

Food and wine matching – don't you just love it? Well, no, actually. I absolutely loathe the subject with a passion I normally reserve for musicals and air travel. While most of my wine-writing counterparts continue to milk this bizarre form of gastronomic blind date ('Mr Riesling, can I introduce you to Miss Thai Curry?') for all it's worth, I continue to swim against the tide of cross-flavour-dressing opinion.

Breaking the same old rules

The mantra of today's gastro-Cillas is 'anything goes' and while this might seem like an encouragingly unstructured philosophy it has paved the way for ridiculous experimentation. Wines to go with curry, wines to go with wind-dried tuna and a kumquat salsa... there is no food-and-wine-matching Everest that hasn't been scaled.

The writer begins by saying there are no rules, that 'anything goes', and that he/she recently broke all the rules by matching a welterweight Shiraz with a lightweight seafood terrine. Then, as if suddenly struck my amnesia, the same author proceeds to list lots of 'dos and don'ts'. At least Hugh Johnson puts a bit of irony into the food and wine section of his *Pocket Wine Book 1997* , advising his readers that 'The British banger requires a 2.5-year-old NE Italian Merlot.' Please, tell me you were being ironic, Hugh.

When you compare different authors' opinions on the subject, you quickly realize how confusing and meaningless this subjective minefield can be. I once checked out three different guides to see what wine went with goats cheese and ended up with a list that included sparkling Shiraz, Saumur-Champigny, Chinon, Australian Cabernet Sauvignon and California Zinfandel. Not much consensus of opinion there, I think you'll agree.

Mission impossible

In restaurants, the whole thing becomes even more ludicrous. Putting aside the fact that deciphering a wine list is frightening enough without worrying about matchmaking, there's the small issue of everyone eating different dishes (each with about five different flavours in it). The idea that you can pair one wine with it all is ludicrous. I go out to eat in order to enjoy myself, not to try and pass some sort of gastronomic exam.

Yes, okay, every wine tastes slightly different when mixed with food, but the differences are enough to warrant a few column inches, not entire books. In my humble opinion, most modern wines go with most modern food, and as long as you use common sense (a big, buttery Chardonnay with oysters, for example, is never going to work), the best thing to do is to dive in and experiment.

If you are absolutely intent on hooking up gastronomic partnerships, however, then there's a valid case for arguing that you should choose whatever wine you want first and then work out what food goes with it.

At a time when the food we eat is becoming far more complex in its combinations of flavour and texture, and the wines we drink increasingly similar in style, a reversal of the normal food-and-wine-matching rules would seem the most appropriate course of action.

Confused? Well, don't worry too much about it. There's always the 'back-label law' to fall back on. After all, most wines 'go well with grilled meats, pasta and cheese'.

Tasting it

THE ESSENTIAL WINE-TASTING KIT

One glass
Tasting wine straight out of the bottle is tricky (noses don't fit into necks very easily), so it's worth investing in a good set of glasses. Thanks to an Austrian called Mr Riedel, there are now lots of beautiful models out there, but there is also a lot of glass snobbery. Personally, I don't think it matters what shape or how expensive your glasses are, just as long as you can swirl without ruining the carpets.

Two hands
Without a couple of these you're going to find opening, pouring and swirling rather tricky.

A pair of eyes
You can tell a lot about a wine just by looking at it. A full-bodied, concentrated wine will be darker than a light, dilute one. An old red wine will have light, tawny edges, a young red won't. An old Chardonnay will look darker and more golden than a young one. An oxidized wine will have a brownish tinge. A high-alcohol wine will leave thick tears on the sides of the glass. So, after nothing more than a good, long stare, you should be able to make some quite accurate judgments about a wine's age, condition and style.

A nose
This is your most important tool – not just for smelling the wine, but for tasting it, too. Try drinking a glass of Mouton-Rothschild when you've got a heavy cold and you might as well be drinking Mouton-Cadet. Your own nose will tell you about the wine's 'nose' (its smell) and the wine's nose will tell you a lot about the wine. It will pick out different aromas (fruits, flowers, everything but – hopefully not – the kitchen sink) which should give you hints about the grape variety, the place the wine came from, and whether it has sat in an oak barrel for a while. It will also tell you whether this wine has simple smells (a cheap, young wine), complicated smells (an expensive, old wine) or nasty smells (a faulty wine).

And as all of you who have tried the 'water down the nostrils' trick will know, the nose and mouth are interconnected, so even when the wine is sloshing around inside, the nose will be working away trying to pick out flavours.

A tongue

Having taken a swig of wine into your mouth, the tongue now takes over the baton. The tip of the tongue is sensitive to sweetness, the sides to acidity, and the back to bitterness, so as soon as some vino washes over these points, you'll get a fairly instant report on what sort of wine it is: a bone-dry, high-acid Riesling from Germany, for instance, or a sweet dessert wine from Australia. The tongue will also detect the weight and texture of a wine, and in particular, it will feel the various sweet, bitter, viscous, and warm sensations produced by alcohol.

A set of gums

All red wines have varying degrees of tannin – that dry, astringent substance that comes from the skins of the grapes – and you'll feel these most on the sides of the mouth and the gums. Most wines these days have far softer textures than they used to. In some cases, the tannin is so unnoticeable you may as well be drinking a red-stained white wine. Occasionally, however, you'll come across a big, tannic monster and your mouth will feel like it has just been swabbed with blotting paper and tea bags.

One good memory

Judging a wine is all about making comparisons with previous drinking experiences. If you've got the memory of an elephant, you'll be able to download hundreds of old wine files every time you take a sip and compare what's in your mouth with what's in your head. If you've got a memory like a sieve (like me), a little notebook comes in very handy.

Spotting great wine

We all know what an average bottle of wine smells and tastes like, but would we know an amazing wine if it landed between our gums? After all, there are lots of sexily dressed premium impostors out there.

Looking at the wine won't help you much. In the glass, an expensive Sauternes doesn't look radically different from a cheap sticky from Australia; the first sign of something extraordinary comes only when you stick your snout in the glass.

An average wine will smell of two or three different elements, and as soon as you've recognized them, you'll have moved on to the sipping bit. A wine in the premier league, on the other hand, will have scents that make the hairs on the back of your neck stand up and your brain shout, 'Oh my God – what's *that*?' It will smell so good you'll find yourself involuntarily twirling the glass and – yes, this might seem a little strange – you won't feel like drinking it straight away. A mild state of hypnosis might set in; then suddenly, you'll feel like Rocky after he's run up the steps and punched his arms in the air.

In your mouth, you'll know definitely that something different is going on. Tasters call it 'mouthfeel', and when a wine is very good, the overriding sensation is one of texture rather than flavour.

By now, it will feel like you've won the world cup (with you scoring the winning goal, of course) and days after you've swallowed the last drop, you'll still be getting crystal-clear action replays of all the best bits.

There is another way of telling when an out-of-body wine experience is heading your way: when you look at the bill and have an out-of-wallet experience.

Classic signs that you've been touched by greatness
- Your rate of drinking slows down.
- You feel high.
- You suddenly find yourself surrounded by thirsty friends.
- You write your first tasting note.
- You swear allegiance to *terroir* after years of knocking *terroirists*.
- You drink the whole bottle yourself but don't get a hangover.
- You insist on keeping the empty bottle.

Spotting duff wine

Just as milk can go off and beer can go flat, so wine can have its bad days, too. Fortunately, the number of faulty wines out there is relatively small, but occasionally you will come across a real stinker and you are well within your rights to return the bottle to the sommelier or to the shop at which you bought it.

There are grey areas, of course, and there are many cases where one man's faulty wine is another one's beautiful, complex creation.

Houston, we have a problem

THE WINE HAS A BROWNISH TINGE A good sign that the wine has oxidized and that it will taste dull and flat.

THE LEVEL OF THE WINE IN THE BOTTLE IS LOW AND THE CORK IS VERY WET A good sign that the cork didn't fit properly and the wine is likely to be oxidized.

THE WINE SMELLS LIKE SHERRY EVEN THOUGH IT ISN'T SHERRY Yes, it's Mr Oxidation again; time to throw out the bottle.

THE WINE SMELLS LIKE MUSHROOMS AND MOULD Your wine has been contaminated by a chemical called TCA, and it is now what is known as 'corked'.

THE WINE SMELLS LIKE VINEGAR Either you've picked up the wrong bottle or your wine is heading towards fish-and-chip material.

THE WINE CAUSES A SHARP BURNING SENSATION IN YOUR NOSE, RESULTING IN SUDDEN SNEEZING This is caused by sulphur dioxide, which is used to preserve the wine. In small doses, it should blow off with a bit of contact with air.

Mission control, everything's okay

SOME WHITE WINES REVEAL TINY BUBBLES WHEN YOU PULL THE CORK A slight spritz (due to dissolved carbon dioxide) is perfectly normal in certain young wines.

SOME RED WINES HAVE A LARGE AMOUNT OF SEDIMENT IN THE BOTTLE This is just a sign that the wine hasn't been overfiltered.

SOME WINES SMELL OF CAT'S PEE Odd, but perfectly acceptable in New Zealand Sauvignon Blanc.

SOME WHITE WINES HAVE LITTLE WHITE CRYSTALS IN THE BOTTOM OF THE BOTTLE These are just harmless tartrate deposits, and won't have any affect on the taste of the wine.

The great wine-storage game

Under the bed
Having your wine lying down close to where you lie down might seem a good idea, but a little too much nocturnal activity could send a few too many vibrations through your claret collection.

In the airing cupboard
If you want to turn all your wines into Madeira, this is a great place to keep them. If you don't, then make it a fluffy-towel-only zone.

Near to babies and small children
Wine is a delicate thing. It doesn't like to be shaken up, dropped or have its labels peeled off or graffitied. So treat it like medicine and keep it out of reach of children.

In the bathroom
Gazing at your Romanée-Conti as you lie back in the bath might seem the perfect way to relax, but with all that steam your labels won't last long.

In the conservatory

Plenty of space in here, but direct sunlight and the greenhouse effect will leave your wine more stewed than Auntie's casserole.

In the kitchen

Unless you are planning on drinking the stuff soon, this will be far too warm. Plus, there's always the danger that someone will mistakenly use the Lafite for the Boeuf Bourguignonne.

In the garage

'Now this'll be a nice cool place to store my wine,' you think. And then the first cold snap arrives and you find your Grange has turned into a Shiraz ice lolly.

Under the stairs

It might be the oldest storage cliché in the book, but the pokey cupboard with the vacuum cleaner and ironing board is still the best place to keep your wine if you haven't got a cellar. Dark and relatively cool.

Saving it

One of the stranger habits of the wine community (apart from spitting out rather than swallowing their drinks) is the tendency of its members to buy far more wine than they need. Why, you might rightly ask, would anyone want to set up a bottle shop under the stairs when there's a perfectly good one just down the road? Why sit around waiting for 10 years for a wine to become drinkable when there are thousands of wines out there that are ready to drink now? These are very logical lines of questioning, and yes, this habit does bring out the very worst in the hunter-gatherer/possessive-recluse side of our characters. Yet we only have to present one item of evidence to convince the non-believers that laying down wine is a good idea. Get them to taste a really good bottle of old wine and there is no way they'll ever accuse us of space-wasting domestic crimes again. Get them to smell a 40-year-old burgundy or taste the velvety smoothness of a mature claret and maybe – just maybe – they'll understand (if not admire) this bizarre, patience-testing ritual. Besides its potentially damaging effects on steady relationships, the main problem with keeping wine is finding an appropriate place to stash the stuff.

HOW TO START A CELLAR WITHOUT A CELLAR

Wine is a delicate and fussy thing. It dislikes excess light, wild swings in temperatures and vibration, but it does like a bit of humidity (to stop the corks from drying out) and a nice, horizontal position. A cellar is therefore the obvious choice, but in these days of loft-living singletons and basement conversions, the chances of you having a dark underground space are as slim as you having the financial resources to fill it.

The Japanese reckon they've found a novel solution to this problem, which involves speeding up the ageing process by sending sound vibrations through the wine. It's called the Bodysonic Wine Improver. Having tracked one down and put it through its paces in my living room, unfortunately I have to report that the little noisy box made no difference to my wine and a lot of difference (thanks to its incessant droning) to my sanity.

Storage options

So how do you start building up a cellar when you haven't got a cellar? Depending on your budget and the sort of wine you intend to keep, there are a number of options available.

If you intend to drink the wine within a few years, the bottle costs less than the price of a CD and you find a place with reasonably stable temperature (ergo: not the kitchen), then keeping the wine at home shouldn't be a problem.

If you want to keep it a bit longer and the bottle costs more than 10 CDs, you might want to invest in one of those special temperature-controlled wine holders. And if you're looking to leave it for the long-haul and the bottle costs more

than your CD player, you should definitely consider using the wine equivalent of dog kennels. Just as with canines, leaving your wine in the hands of someone else makes some people a bit nervous, and storage warehouses vary enormously. When I recently checked my wine – kept at one of London's largest storage centres – I was amazed to find bright sunlight pouring through the windows and no temperature control. I have since found a new home for my wine.

So check the conditions, check the security, check your cases of wine are all individually labelled with your own name and code, then you can sleep soundly. Okay, so you can't just get up in the middle of the night and go and look at your wine (another strange male habit), but at least you know it'll be in prime condition and no one but you can get access to it. Besides, if you've ever heard the story about the jilted wife who delivered her husband's beloved wine collection to the doorsteps of the local community, you'll appreciate the dangers of keeping your wine at home.

Laying down wine

REDS

Taste a young Bordeaux red when it's fresh out of its post-fermentation nappies and you'll find it hard to see how such a tough, aggressive, loud-mouthed baby will ever become something beautiful.

But, amazingly, it does. With a bit of solitude, quiet, and cool, damp conditioning, the ugly little monster transforms itself into a character that is totally unrecognizable from the youngster that left your gums numb, your teeth battered and your tongue in a state of tannic turmoil.

How it happens is a bit of a mystery. The things that go on inside a bottle of wine are still just as debatable as the internal workings of the Mir space station. We can see that things are going on, we can make some basic assumptions about how those things happened, but when it comes down to specifics, even the experts are left floundering.

What we do know is that as red wines age, they react with oxygen and change colour from deep ruby-purple to brick-red and tawny. We also know they become softer as the tannins (those astringent, dry substances that come from grape skins) change shape and bond together. They begin to smell and taste very different, and in some cases they change prices rather radically.

The tricky (and fun) part is working out at what point during this metamorphosis you should open a bottle of wine and start drinking it. Too many people think it's some sort of endurance test and end up asking 'How long should I keep it?' rather than 'When should I drink it?' Peak drinking time is often short, so if in doubt, drink earlier rather than later.

Red caterpillars
- Bordeaux (claret)
- Burgundy and New World Pinot Noir
- Barolo
- Tuscan reds
- Top California Zinfandel and Cabernet Sauvignon
- Rhône blends and Australian Shiraz

WHITES

Far too many cellars have a discriminatory door policy. The big blokes dressed in red – with full bodies and tannins bulging out of their T-shirts – always get welcomed in without question, while the lads in white are refused entry and sent back to the drink-it-young club. It's a strange colour prejudice to have. Not only are there lots of white-wine styles that benefit from ageing, but on the basis that you keep wines to see them change outfits, white wines give you far more makeovers per year than the red bunch.

While a big Rhône Syrah might have softened and evolved after a decade in the dark, a German Riesling will come out with a brand-new colour, aroma, texture and weight. Unlike reds – which use a tannic Zimmer frame to lean on – whites rely primarily on acidity to get them into the OAP club. Acidity is the backbone holding the wine's body together; without it, you'll just end up with a flabby old thing that boasts all the structure of a Dali clock.

Also unlike reds – which tend to become paler as the years go by – whites turn darker, and the journey towards maturity can be more of a rollercoaster ride than the relatively predictable development of the red-cellar brigade. White Châteauneuf-du-Pape, for example, often has a two-year sulk cycle where it pretends to be dead and buried and then surprises everyone by sitting up straight a year later. Aussie Semillon does something similar by having a mid-life crisis before settling down and re-emerging full of life as if nothing ever happened.

Yet while keeping a white-wine cellar might require a bit more nerve and greater skill in judging when to open the bottle, the rewards of treading this riskier path are great.

White caterpillars
- Burgundy
- Sweet Bordeaux (especially Sauternes)
- German Riesling
- Loire whites
- Alsace Gewürztraminer
- Australian Hunter Valley Semillon

How wines age: charting the unchartable

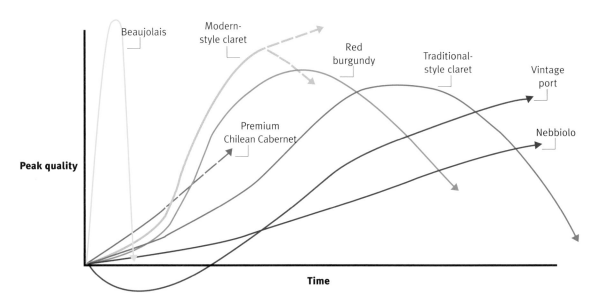

Beaujolais

Modern-
style claret

Red
burgundy

Traditional-
style claret

Vintage
port

Premium
Chilean Cabernet

Nebbiolo

Peak quality

Time

Red-wine maturity chart

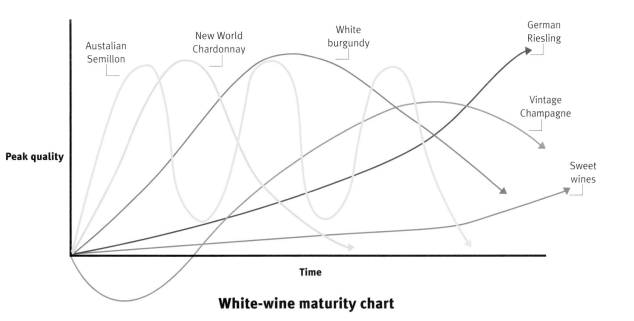

Peak quality

Austalian
Semillon

New World
Chardonnay

White
burgundy

German
Riesling

Vintage
Champagne

Sweet
wines

Time

White-wine maturity chart

Spirits, or Prada, Paul Smith & Patrón

If you want to remind yourself what real humiliation feels like, walk into a reasonably stylish bar in New York City and say in a loud, clear voice, 'I'll have a vodka, please.' The bartender will initially give you one of those slightly disbelieving smiles – you know, the one the Hell's Angel biker gives when the manager of the diner asks him to move his bike from the disabled parking slot. And then he'll ask you what you want again, and – thinking he must be a few limes short of a full Caipirinha – you'll repeat loudly, 'A VODKA, PLEASE.' Eventually, after the laughter dies down and people stop staring, the barman will say nice and slowly, 'We have 40 different brands of clear anaesthetic, sir. I'll need something a little more specific than just "vodka".' Welcome to a new age of spirit appreciation, where failure to name the names can leave you very embarrassed and very thirsty.

This little nightmare scenario is an exaggerated (but accurate) warning that a) spirits have become extremely fashionable again, and b) people are becoming just as choosy about the label they drink as they are about the designer glasses they wear in order to see the label in the first place. Just as you hear people saying they wear Prada, smoke Cohibas and celebrate with Bolly, you now find those same people saying they sip Patrón, mix Myers and freeze Krolewska.

Off the back of the wine boom with its deference for *terroir* has come a growing thirst for authentic spirits with a story behind the label. Single-malt whiskies, sipping Tequilas, boutique rums, small-batch Bourbons, higher-strength gins… all of these have benefited from the surge in interest in carefully made, distinct, original spirits. But don't worry if you don't know your Rain from your Ketel One. Regardless of what some spirits snobs (they're like overproof wine bores) might say or sniff at, there is no right or wrong choice in the optics fashion stakes. After all, one man's Plymouth is another man's Tanqueray just as Patrón is Tequila heaven to one person and overhyped agave juice to another. The only bar-crime you will get lynched for is not caring what you drink; the choice is wider than ever, so make the most of it.

The tasteless fashion parade

Vodka: flavourless anaesthetic for the comfortably numb generation

Defining it

Vodka is a basic commodity used by Poles and Russians as a form of escapism and cold-weather insulation. If you live in the West, however, then it's a status symbol for style-bar-loafing badge-drinkers.

Making it

Choose a type of grain such as barley, wheat or rye. Add water (the cleaner and purer the better) and yeast and then heat and stir until the mixture ferments and creates a type of beer. If you can't find any grain, improvise and use potatoes (or anything that contains starch). Distil your alcoholic brew, preferably in a continuous-column still for extra purity. Either sweeten and add flavour to taste, or simply filter through charcoal, dilute to the required strength, garnish with authentically roughed-up Eastern European packaging and serve to impressionable 20-somethings.

Tasting it

Yes, vodka *does* have flavour, and no, not all vodkas taste the same. Good grain vodkas will actually try to use the character of the grain to distinguish themselves from other products. Flavours you are likely to encounter include vanilla, anise, sweetcorn, rye, pepper and chocolate. A hot, spicy (almost chilli-esque) finish is a bad sign: good-quality vodka will not have a harsh, alcoholic bite.

Drinking it

The advice I was given by two army veterans at London's Polish Centre (the best location for serious vodka research) was that vodka 'must be very cold, it must be drunk in one swift swallow, and it is best with food'. In Eastern Europe, you will commonly drink vodka throughout a meal (it goes very well with salty and pickled dishes) as if it were wine, and many Russians actually drink it out of what look like Champagne flutes. In the West, we tend to use it as a cocktail base, but despite the versatility offered by flavourlessness, I think most vodka cocktails would taste far better if another spirit were used as the base.

Experiencing it

Served straight from the freezer, vodka slips down in a smooth-gliding, viscous stream, creating an afterglow that only the finest neat injection can achieve.

To get that essential vodka experience, you really need to be sitting around a table in a hunting cabin somewhere in Siberia with a gale howling outside, a room full of large, inebriated Russians as your only company, and a plentiful supply of Igor's home-distilled potato special. If that doesn't appeal, you might like to visit your nearest style bar and shoot shots of the latest triple-distilled super-premium brand.

Speaking it

NAZDROWIE/NAZDOROVYE The classic Polish/Russian toast, which literally means 'your health'.
CONGENERS Chemical compounds that give vodka its taste and smell.
VODKA Means 'little water'. Sometimes spelled 'wodka'.
GOLDWASSER A digestif vodka made with herbs, spices and gold leaf.
BISON GRASS A wild herb used to make a particular type of flavoured Polish vodka.
RECTIFIED SPIRIT Vodka bottled at distillation strength.

Reinventing it

Not that long ago, ordering a vodka in a bar was deemed to be about as fashionable as creased jeans. But then along came Absolut and all its flavoured pals; suddenly, it was alright to be all white. Today, vodka is selling itself as much on flavour as it is on purity. The drink once considered to be a working-class staple in some countries is now reinventing itself as a super-premium product with a price tag not quite so cool as the spirit itself.

The classic vodka drink: The Vodka Martini

Gin-drinking traditionalists might moan that this is *their* cocktail, but it is the vodka version that has put the Martini back on the style-bar map. Although simple to make, this drink is also easy to make badly. Take a cocktail glass from the freezer and add a couple of drops of vermouth before pouring in your preferred brand of vodka (it must also be from the freezer) and garnishing with an olive. Preferably not stirred, definitely not shaken, the Vodka Martini (or Vodkatini) is one helluva neat 'n' naked way to start the evening.

CHOOSING VODKA

Polish vodka: Wyborowa

The Poles take their national spirit very seriously and treat drinking vodka as an important social event. There are over 1,000 brands available (choosing a vodka in a Polish supermarket can be a lengthy process), rye tends to be the favoured grain, and the best versions are full-flavoured with hints of rye bread and nuts.

Russian vodka: Moskovskaya

Russians would argue that life wouldn't be bearable without vodka, yet Russia as an economic force would undoubtedly be in a better state if it didn't exist. It is both a blessing and a curse. The collapse of communism has allowed some of the best brands to reach foreign markets, but economic disintegration has meant some slips in quality (sometimes with disastrous consequences for the drinker).

Scandinavian vodka: Absolut

Wheat and barley are more widely used in Scandinavia, and the vodka is lighter in flavour compared with its Polish and Russian counterparts. The most famous is Absolut (Sweden), a wheat-based, slightly sweet vodka that took the drinks world by storm, thanks to one of the most successful advertising campaigns ever launched. Other brands to look for are Finlandia, Danzka and Seriously.

Fashion-victim's vodka: Grey Goose

Heritage and history are no longer required for vodka to be successful; exclusivity, word-of-mouth marketing and quality are the three key ingredients. Take Grey Goose. It is an ultra-premium French vodka made from a blend of four grains and pure mineral water. From a standing start in 1997, it now sells over half a million cases a year in the US.

Neutral vodka: Skyy

Most vodkas made outside vodka's historical heartlands are relatively neutral in character. Some, like Grey Goose, are extremely good products. Others are – well, let's just say the words 'Lada' and 'fuel' spring to mind. Many inferior ones are made in the same distilleries that make neutral spirit for gin production.

Organic vodka: Rain

Organic vodka might not taste any different from non-organic vodka and there are no guarantees your hangover will be environmentally friendly, but at least you can drink with a clear conscience. Rain is made from organically grown American grain and pure Kentucky limestone water. After quadruple distillation and diamond-dust filtration, you could say it's as clean as a whistle.

Aged vodka: Polish Starka

Bored with yet another neutral flavour (or perhaps just bored, full stop), the Poles and Russians have been known to lay down vodka in empty wine casks for up to 10 years. Sometimes a small amount of wine, port or brandy is added to the vodka before ageing.

Flavoured vodka: Zubrowka

Flavoured vodkas are not a new invention; such was the poor quality of early vodkas that flavouring was a necessity rather than an option. Thanks to brands like Absolut, however, they have become far more mainstream. Some might argue that the proliferation of cucumbers, peppers and fruits has taken this style from the sublime to the ridiculous, but they have certainly added a valuable string of weapons to the cocktail-maker's arsenal.

The wine-taster's vodka: Seriously

You might think there is nothing else that can be done with vodka, but you'd be forgetting those Swedish guys with their strange sauna habits and far too much time on their hands. Seriously is a brand created (so the hype says) by a bunch of wine experts who wanted a vodka that didn't have an alcoholic bite. Despite really wanting to dislike it purely on grounds of it being a daft concept, it's actually not a bad little drop of spirit.

Geographically ambiguous vodka: Smirnoff

While other spirits stress the importance of where a product is made, vodka carries no such pretensions. Smirnoff, for example, is a locally produced vodka, so despite its pretence at being Russian, you'll find that the British version is actually distilled in Scotland.

The birth of Tequila

Tequila: the best legal buzz you can get

Defining it

Tequila is the secret weapon invented by Mexicans to reduce productivity in other economies. It is also a spirit made by distilling the fermented juice of the blue agave plant.

Making it

Take one mature blue agave plant. Trim off its excess foliage and cut out the sweet, juicy bit, known in Spanish as the *piña*, or 'pineapple'. Slice each *piña* into four portions and bake for 24 to 48 hours in order to release the plant's sugars. Crush the mixture to release the sap and transfer to a non-stick vat for fermentation. Add cane sugar if you wish to make a 'mixed' Tequila (all Tequila must by law contain at least 51 percent agave spirit), or leave undiluted if making a 100 percent agave version. Distil twice and either transfer to barrels for ageing (*reposado/añejo*) or release straight away as *joven/blanco*-style Tequila. Will serve large groups of gringos.

Tasting it

The bad stuff can seem as unpalatable as aviation fuel, but good Tequila has a character that flits somwhere between the sweet appeal of a Bourbon and the smoky, salty flavours of malt whisky.

Drinking it

There are four main ways Tequila is served: as a shot, as a slammer, as a cocktail and as a digestif/aperitif to be sipped and savoured. Shots – usually delivered by someone wearing glass-bearing bullet belts and a knowing smile – require the assistance of a pinch of salt between thumb and forefinger and a wedge of lime. The two act as a sort of anaesthetic to mask the taste of cheap Tequila and prevent what went down from coming back up.

Slamming involves mixing Tequila with lemon juice and something fizzy (sparkling wine or soda water), then testing the strength of your glass on the table and the strength of your will by knocking it back in one. Tequila cocktails (Margaritas, Tequila Sunrises, etc) treat the spirit with a little more respect. Finally, you can follow the latest American fad and sip aged Tequila like you would a single-malt whisky.

Experiencing it

We've all done it (haven't we?). We've all had that Tequila experience where large chunks (or in some cases, entire nights) fail to reappear when we press the total-recall button the following morning, and we've all sworn blind that there must be some weird ingredient that causes such memory loss. Whether you blame the agave or the mad way in which you drink the stuff, there is no doubt that a Tequila buzz is like no other alcoholic high, and a Tequila hangover is the mother and father of all cranium-crunching experiences.

Speaking it

AÑEJO A term used for golden Tequila that has been in oak for one year or more.

JOVEN As in 'young'. Tequila that has not been matured in oak.

PLATA (SILVER) A clear Tequila that hasn't been oak-aged.

PULQUE The poor man's Tequila. Pulque is simply the fermented sap (some call it 'beer') of the agave plant.

REPOSADO A 'rested' Tequila that has been matured in oak casks for between 60 days and a year.

SANGRITA A cocktail made with Tequila and tomato juice; a Tequila Bloody Mary.

100% AGAVE If this is what it says on the label, then that is what they made it from.

Reinventing it

Despite its downmarket slamming side, Tequila has become the most fashionable sipping material on the style-bar circuit. With double shots of cult *añejos* now bearing triple-figure price tags and celebs getting stroppy if their Patrón is not available, asking for a Tequila now gets you a nod of respect rather than a request for your ID card.

The classic Tequila drink: The Margarita

In essence, the Margarita is just a rich man's version of the lick, gulp and suck routine. Like the shot-glass sensation, the salt – this time around the rim of the glass – is the first thing you taste, while the bite of fresh citrus-fruit juice is there to help the Tequila go down. A dash of triple sec or Cointreau bonds the whole thing together.

CHOOSING TEQUILA

The Tequila found everywhere: José Cuervo Especial

Walk into any bar in the world and there are strong odds of finding a bottle of Cuervo Gold. Made in industrial quantities, with caramel added for flavour and colour, this gives good alcohol but not much else. Slammer and shot material.

The Tequila for great Margaritas: Herradura Blanco 100% agave

Allegedly, Bing Crosby first brought this into the US, shipping it over the border in bulk to fuel his parties. It's dry and spicy, with the earthy taste of agave coming through strongly and a pleasant peppery kick to end.

The Tequila for the Bourbon drinker: José Cuervo Añejo

With its strong aromas and flavours of vanilla, caramel and coconut, there's a strong hint of Jim Beam in this Tequila. A nice, gentle opener for the Tequila-sipping novice.

The Tequila a Mexican would order: Cazadores Reposado

From language students in London to vineyard workers in California, an exile's eyes will light up if he walks into a bar and sees the bottle with a stag on the label. Smooth and spicy, with a flavour that makes you want to start a Mexican wave.

The Tequila for the open-minded drinker: Chinaco Añejo

Traditionalists in the Tequila-making heartlands were more than a little miffed when this company began distilling in an offshoot region called Tamaulipes. The result is a very distinct, quite vegetal/earthy-style drink that proves there's *terroir* in Tequila as well as wine.

The Tequila with a split personality: Corralejo Reposado

This starts off light and elegant, with a soothing call of *venga, mi amigo*. Then you swallow. Suddenly, Eli Wallach has just ridden into your village and there's fire everywhere. Where are the Magnificent Seven when you really need them?

The Tequila the Hollywood director would order: Patrón Añejo

An American-owned, ultra-premium brand that has built up a fanatical following on the A-list celeb circuit. The squat, hand-blown bottle might look cute, but this little baby acts like a real prizefighter when it gets to work on your gums.

The Tequila for the fashion victim: Porfidio Single-Barrel Añejo

Trendy blue, ceramic containers and bottles with glass cacti inside make Porfidio the number-one choice for label buyers. It's a good Tequila, but don't try ordering it in downtown Guadalajara.

The rich man's Tequila: 1800 Colección

Just as northern Italians must scratch their heads in bemusement at the prices rich people pay for trendy grappas, Mexican workers must laugh at the idea of gringos forking out megabucks for their local drink. Of the growing number of small-production, beautifully packaged Tequilas hitting the market, Cuervo Colección is the mother and father of all overpriced shots. Only 347 bottles of this special release were made, and for the price of a bottle in New York, you could probably host a week-long party in Mexico.

Mezcal: Lajita, Monte Alban, Hacienda Sotol

While Tequila is the drink of city bars and suited-up executives, mezcal is the spirit of rural communities and the machete-wielding *piña*-cutters. This is the first of many differences. Tequila is distilled in and around the state of Jalisco, while mezcal comes predominantly from the southern state of Oaxaca. Tequila is made from blue agave, mezcal can be made from a wide variety of strains of the desert lily. Mezcal production involves steaming or boiling the *piñas* before extracting juice, but with mezcal they are slow-roasted in adobe ovens to give the spirit its distinctive smoky flavour. Traditionally, bottles of mezcal have contained a *gusano* (the larva of a butterfly, not a worm) that, thanks to movie legend and folklore, has a reputation for having hallucinogenic properties. Sorry to disappoint you, but it's nothing more than a gimmick.

Gin: the quintessential English spirit

Defining it

According to your point of view and age, gin is either a drink that takes a neutral spirit and skilfully ties flavours to it or it is simply juniper-flavoured vodka. Either way, the Queen Mother reached 100 years on it, middle England swears by it, and Martini-lovers get their slick, cold kicks from it.

Making it

First, take some neutral spirit, preferably made from grain, not molasses. Second, choose your botanicals (juniper, coriander, citrus-fruit peel, angelica root, cassia bark, etc) with the only provisos being that a) juniper is the greatest in volume, and b) your recipe is different from the ones owned and operated by your rivals.

Third, mix in these aromatics by re-distilling your neutral spirit with the botanicals either suspended over the rising vapour (racking) or dunked *à la* tea bag (steeping) in the liquid itself. Dilute to an appropriate strength and serve to little old ladies and retired army captains.

Tasting it

Gin is one of the most aromatic and distinctive spirits in the world. In childhood, the smell of Gordon's signalled to me that Dad was home from work. As an adult, it never fails to trigger memories of lazy summer evenings and holidays past. The key flavour is obviously juniper, followed by various layers of citrus fruit, liquorice, cinnamon, coriander and almond, according to the botanicals used.

Drinking it

All spirits have their peak drinking hours. Bourbon and Scotch come into their own late at night, Tequila hits the soft spot best at about 8pm and a digestif like grappa comes somewhere midway between the two. Gin, on the other hand, is definitely an early evening, watch-the-sun-go-down type of drink. Singapore Slings, Martinis, and Gin & Tonics have always been the building blocks on which a great night is built rather than the parting shots at its inglorious finale.

Experiencing it

It may be a British spirit, but to get the Full Monty Martini moment, you have to go to New York and the 5757 bar at The Four Seasons Hotel. Dress to impress (gin-drinking requires a certain sartorial elegance), make sure dinner is booked and transport is on hand, then order a Martini and prepare to drift away in a lovely fuzzy haze of confident indifference.

Alternatively, head for the tropics, find an old colonial joint (most mosquito-infested destinations have one) and sit on the terrace with a long, cold Gin & Tonic.

Speaking it

BOTANICALS The plant-based ingredients that give gin its flavour.

PINK GIN Gin mixed with Angostura bitters. Believe it or not, it was invented as a medicine by the surgeons of the Royal Navy.

LONDON DRY GIN A style of gin, not a stamp of origin.

OLD TOM GIN A sweet style of gin rarely found today.

GENEVER The old Dutch name for gin. The word originally meant 'juniper', and was what the Dutch called the spirit they invented and passed on to the thirsty English.

Reinventing it

Unfortunately, gin suffers from the 'don't drink what your dad does' syndrome, and it may have to wait a while before a new generation of gin-drinkers comes through. Mind you, strong efforts are being made (by Plymouth, among others) to sell gin as a versatile cocktail base.

The classic gin drink: The Gin & Tonic

The sad facts are these: the drink that lubricated the administrative cogs of the British Empire returned home after years of hard, tropical service and instead of receiving a hero's welcome, found itself being treated with the greatest disrespect. Poorly made and badly served, it became a permanent member of the abused and neglected drinks club. So let's try and straighten things out. It helps if you start with a decent gin at a decent strength (yes, there is life beyond Gordon's), add cold tonic from a fresh (not half-used) bottle, ice, a couple of wedges of lime (squeeze some of the juice in first) and a dash of Angostura bitters. *Et voila*: a G&T with length, strength and class.

CHOOSING GIN

The one your dad drinks: Gordon's

Ever since Gordon's dropped its alcohol level to 37.5 percent – in gin circles, a crime akin to leaking your botanical recipe to a competitor – the world's biggest-selling gin has not exactly been top of the bartender's 'favourite brands' list. It is one of the lightest gins and has pronounced juniper and citrus-fruit flavours. Nevertheless, middle-aged middle England still loves it, and most of the world's Gin & Tonics are made with it.

The one still made in London: Beefeater

There is no doubt that a large part of Beefeater's success is due to its British branding (a sense of Britishness is important to some gin-drinkers), but it is also thanks to its superb quality and strong reputation in bartending circles. I find this a very citric gin, and it makes a mean Martini.

The one with organic ingredients: Juniper Green

Charles Maxwell, head of Thames Distillers, didn't find it too difficult to track down organic botanicals, but it took him over a year to find a supplier of organic spirit. Now some of you might wonder why anyone would bother going to such trouble (let's face it, spirit is pretty pure stuff regardless of where the grain comes from), but sales of Juniper Green suggest otherwise. And with organic tonic water now available, the green G&T is here at last.

The one in the round green bottle: Tanqueray

This rich, full-flavoured gin comes in two strengths (43 percent and 47 percent) and is easily recognized by its very seductive coriander and juniper flavours and full-bodied weight in the mouth. If ever you needed evidence that alcohol is crucial to the balance of botanicals, a taste of Tanqueray is it. Look out for the triple-distilled Tanqueray Malacca – a spicier brand that feels more East Indies than East London.

The one that 'allegedly' made the original Dry Martini: Plymouth

Being a regular guest at the captain's table, Plymouth once got to parts of the world other gins failed to reach. Changing ownership left it floundering for a while, but it is now back to full strength in all senses of the word. Here is a brand that offers at least four different flavours, with no one single botanical overpowering the other. Absolut recently took a large stake in the business, so Plymouth's distribution might get back to what it once was.

The one with a lot of botanicals: Bombay Sapphire

What it lacks in history it makes up for in striking packaging and great marketing. On the botanical front it's a case of everything from orris root to cubeb berries being used to flavour the spirit. So don't spoil all that effort by adding tonic to it.

The one with the whisky connection: Gloag's

Scotch whisky to gin might seem like a large corporate hop, but Matthew Gloag has shown it isn't a hop too far. Like Bombay, Gloag's gin uses a long list of botanicals. The end result is a spirit with strong aromatics and a peppery kick in the mouth.

The one they call genever: Dutch Gin

They might have been the inspiration for British versions, but Dutch gins have never enjoyed much international success. With their heavier spirit bases and predominant use of juniper, they taste and feel very different, and in the case of the old straw-coloured, slightly sweet, Oude-style genever, they are almost unrecognizable.

The ones with greater strength: Beefeater Crown Jewel and Plymouth Navy Strength

Alcoholic strength is seen as being a key factor affecting the quality of gin. Most distillers agree that 40 percent abv is the minimum a gin should be and that higher levels can be better for 'holding' the aromas and flavours imparted by the botanicals. But how far should you go? Personally, I find anything in the 43 to 47 percent range ideal, but head over 50 percent (Plymouth Navy Strength is a whopping 57 percent) and you begin to numb the senses and lose the botanical plot.

Rum: shaking off its navy bell-bottoms

Defining it

Rum (or Ron or Rhum) is a spirit produced from sugar cane. Once a pirate's best friend, still a Christmas pudding's worst nightmare, rum wins gold in the spirit Olympics for its wide display of styles, versatility in the mixing department and the best portfolio of distillery-visit destinations.

Making it

Take one large field of sugar cane and chop it down to size. Cut and shred the canes to let their juices flow. Then, using fresh sugar-cane juice, or cane syrup or molasses, add yeast and ferment until you have a nice, alcoholic mash. Place your mash in a still (pot or column, according to the style of rum you want to make) and distil. At this stage, you can either release it as unaged white rum or put it into oak casks to make a golden rum. To make a dark rum you just age it in barrels for longer, for a more mellow (usually lower-alcohol) spirit. Finally, blend and bottle.

Tasting it

With white rum, you can expect to find the flavours of sugar (demerara and muscovado), caramel, vanilla and cinnamon, while at the darker end of the spectrum, you should be getting lost in a nasal whirl of coffee, toffee, chocolate, fudge, and fruits such as banana and orange.

Drinking it

Bacardi & Coke (or Bundy & Coke, if you're drinking Australian) go together as well as gin & tonic or vodka & cranberry. Yet if you're a bit embarrassed to order one, try adding a kick of lime and dash of Cuban kudos with a Cuba Libre. For something a little more testing in the mixology department, you could try a Mojito (Cuban rum, lime, mint and soda water) or Caipirinha (Cachaça rum, limes and sugar) or you could treat your rum with the utmost respect and just sip it neat.

Experiencing it

No matter what those creative types at the Bacardi marketing department might like you to think, a rum drunk in the Dog and Duck on a rainy day in Peckham doesn't leave you with sand between your toes and an Auntie Ethel who looks like Charlize Theron. Sorry, but if you really want that full-on rum effect, you've got to go exotic. A Rum Punch on the beach in Jamaica, a Mojito in Havana's Bodeguita del Medio, a Caipirinha at the carnival in Rio – these are the only truly effective remedies for the high-latitude blues.

Speaking it

AGRICOLE The name for rum produced from sugar-cane juice rather than molasses.

AGUARDENTE DE CANA A distillate made from sugar cane.

MOLASSES The thick, black residue left after sugar crystals have been extracted from cane juice.

DUNDER Residue from the previous distillation used to make a more pungent rum.

OVD A dark, blended rum still widely drunk by grizzly old fishermen in Scotland. The initials (for such they are) mean 'Old Vatted Demerara'.

OVERPROOF Er... it means don't light your cigarette after drinking it.

RUM PUNCH A fruity and refreshing drink made by mixing rum with various fruit juices and soda water.

Reinventing it

There are some who think drinking rum is to fashion what the Royal Navy is to trouser design, and when you see the amount of Captain Morgan still splashed over Christmas pudding and mixed with butter rather than ice, it's hard not to agree. But up in the crow's nest of drink predictions, the words 'trend ahoy' have been heard, and at last this sailor's staple is hoisting up its proverbial mainsail and getting some respect. Dark spirits are about to have their day, and rum is ready to make a noise like a force-six gale off Dogger Bank.

The classic rum drink: The Daiquiri

It has become something of a tourist cliché to visit the Floridita bar in Havana and join the conveyor belt of visitors passing through for their taste of Hemingway's favourite cocktail. But even commercial exploitation can't dilute the appeal of this simple but inspired dash of tropical mixology. White rum, lime juice and some sugar syrup, shaken, strained and sipped.

CHOOSING RUM

The biggest rum in the world: Bacardi

Such has been the marketing success of the world's biggest spirit brand that there are plenty of drinkers out there who believe Bacardi is a type of spirit rather than a brand of rum. When Don Facundo Bacardi Masso established his distillery in Santiago de Cuba in 1862, he began making rums that would completely change the perception of this once-harsh, fiery spirit. Light, easy-drinking rums were born, and cocktail barmen suddenly had a new, versatile base for their art. Most of us come into contact with only the ubiquitous Carta Blanca, but if you can find a bottle of Bacardi 8-year-old, your taste buds are in for a very nice surprise.

White Rum: Appleton White, Wray & Nephew Overproof...

All rums are white (clear) after distillation; colour is obtained by barrel-ageing and/or the addition of caramel. White rums tend to be lighter in style and are normally used as bases for cocktails rather than drunk neat like golden rums.

Golden Rum: Appleton Estate 12-year-old, Mount Gay Eclipse...

The Caribbean islands are home to a wide range of beautiful, gold-coloured rums. These are rums that have been aged in barrels (usually ex-Bourbon casks) and owing to excessive evaporation loss in the humid tropics, the older ones tend to be very rare and very expensive. The rewards for your patience and financial outlay are complex layers of vanilla, toffee, fudge, fruits and muscovado sugar.

Light vs Heavy Rum: Havana Club 3-year-old vs Wood's 100 Old Navy Rum

As well as being divided by colour (white, golden, dark), rum is also split into two weight bands according to the purity to which it is distilled. The fewer congeners (impurities), the lighter the rum; as a general rule, lighter rums seem to come from countries colonized by the Spanish, while heavier styles come from the old British and French colonies. The picture is complicated by the fact that most distillers blend the two.

British Rum: Captain Morgan, Black Heart, OVD, Lamb's...

There is a long history of Caribbean rums being shipped in bulk to Britain to be aged and blended into a dark, treacly style of spirit appreciated more for its warming properties than subtleties of flavour. Despite a hard core of drinkers in Scotland, this type of rum is in danger of becoming a relic of a bygone age.

Cuban Rum: Havana Club

Tourism, Salsa, Buena Vista... Cuba has never been more fashionable, and with Mojitos and Daiquiris sitting high on the style-bar cocktail list, the island's most famous brand of rum is enjoying the spotlight. With an island full of sugar cane and little competition (thanks to Castro's nationalization of the rum industry), you could say life is pretty easy for the Havana Club distillers. But they have never stinted on quality, and if you can get your hands on the 15-year-old (up to £50 a measure in one London bar), then you are in for a revolutionary treat.

Rhum Agricole: J Bally, Clement, Dillon, JM, La Mauny, Damoiseau...

On the islands of Martinique and Guadeloupe, French influence shows itself in both the name for rum (Rhum Agricole) and the strict appellation-style controls on its production. Rhum Agricole is made only from sugar-cane juice, must be distilled in pot stills, and the barrels it is aged in must be of a particular size. These beautifully crafted rums are some of the best in the world: made for slow, 'neat' sipping.

Cachaça: Pitu, Pirassanunga 51, Cana Rio, Germana...

Often referred to as *Aguardente de Cana*, Cachaça is Brazil's national spirit. Thanks to the country's huge population (and thirst), it is one of the biggest-selling spirits in the world. Made from sugar-cane juice, Cachaça is distilled to a lower strength than most rum and thus tends to be more aromatic, full-flavoured and rustic in character. When badly made, you understand why the locals began mixing it with limes, but the best aged versions can be excellent on their own.

Bourbon: a taste of Rhett and Scarlet, or Wild Turkeys all 'round

Defining it

Commonly associated with the Deep South of *Gone with the Wind* fame, the jazz of New Orleans and Memphis, or sometimes with black-and-white pictures of dungaree-wearing men, Bourbon is America's unique spirit and a base for some of the best cocktails in the world.

Making it

Theoretically, you could make Bourbon anywhere (although the name has been registered and protected by the US Congress since 1964, stipulating that it has to be made in the US), just as long as you stayed faithful to a strict set of production regulations. These include using at least 51 percent corn (maize to Europeans) in the grain mix, and ageing your spirit in charred, virgin oak barrels for at least two years. The first thing to do is make up what is known as a mash bill, a mix of different grains that will include corn and usually a combination of malted barley, wheat and rye. Add limestone water to this and heat everything in a pressure cooker until a nice mash is created. Add yeast and some sour mash (*see* 'Speaking it') and ferment to create a beer. Distil the beer into a spirit, put it into a nice, newly charred barrel and leave to mature in a multi-storey warehouse, making sure you rotate its position every so often. After waiting for at least four years, either blend one barrel with lots of others (big-brand Bourbon) or bottle it separately as a small-batch or single-barrel Bourbon.

Tasting it

Cheap, mass-produced Bourbon is nothing more than a lesson in tasting overwooded spirit, but the new wave of small-batch, old-age products offers a smooth, creamy swathe of warm, mellow flavours. Expect to find vanilla, caramel, cinnamon, orange peel, mint, chocolate, wood smoke and dried fruits.

Drinking it

Traditionally – back in the days when you tied your horse up outside the bar and drink-riding wasn't an offence – you'd be poured a little shot glass and back it went in one. Today, Bourbon is usually sipped from tumblers, mixed with water or Coke, or used as the base for cocktails such as Whiskey Sours, Mint Julips and Old Fashioneds.

Experiencing it

For the sophisticated Bourbon experience you could either take yourself to Mardi Gras and soak up some jazz and cocktails in New Orleans, or sip a Mint Julip at the Kentucky Derby. For the unsophisticated, drop into a late-night bar anywhere in the Deep South and play some poker with the local good ol' boys.

Speaking it

KENTUCKY STRAIGHT BOURBON This must be made from a minimum of 51 per cent corn.
SMALL GRAINS The non-corn ingredients (rye, wheat, barley) in Bourbon.
SOUR MASH The yeasty mash taken out from one batch and used to help set off fermentation in the next.
SMALL BATCH Low-production Bourbon bottled from selected casks.
SINGLE BARREL Bourbon bottled from a single cask.
TENNESSEE WHISKEY This is not a Bourbon. From a different state and made differently, these are Bourbon taste-alikes, eg Jack Daniel's,
WHITE DOG The name given to the clear raw spirit that comes out of the stills.

Reinventing it

Facing stiff competition from other spirits, Bourbon has resorted to going upmarket, with small-batch and single-barrel products. From being something you necked down until your hair fell out, it has now turned itself into a complex, sophisticated drink that can be so sublime it makes the hairs on the back of your neck stand up. The day of the sipping Bourbon is upon us (although to those in the know, it never left...).

The classic Bourbon drink: The Mint Julip

Like beer buffs and wine geeks, there is a decidedly nerdy element lurking under the surface of the cocktail-mixing circuit, and the Mint Julip is one of those contentious drinks that brings out the train-spotter in every mixologist. Of the endless permutations available, here is the simplest. Take a few sprigs of fresh mint and muddle them with a shot of sugar syrup in a mixing glass. Add a double shot of Bourbon and some soda water. Stir and pour into a glass of crushed ice. Garnish with mint, and dream of Tara.

CHOOSING BOURBON

The new kid from an old block: Buffalo Trace

A new brand made in one of the oldest distilleries in Kentucky, Buffalo Trace is not widely available outside its home state. Made from batches of no more than 25 to 30 barrels, this is a smooth, warming Bourbon with some attractive sugar and spice notes and a warm, vanilla-streaked finish. A great winter sipper.

The small-batch Bourbon with big-batch distribution: Maker's Mark

Its ubiquity might raise a little scepticism about the term 'small batch', but nevertheless, Maker's Mark gets a thumbs-up from most bartenders I speak to. Made with wheat (rather than rye) as its small grain, it can seem lighter than some of its counterparts, but for its layers of moreish butterscotch and caramel flavours, it definitely gets the crowd-pleasing vote.

The big-brand Bourbon: Jim Beam

For many people Jim Beam is their introduction to Bourbon drinking, and although fairly light in style the white label is still pretty good for a large-production whiskey. The black-label 8-year-old is excellent and the Beam family now make a number of small-batch Bourbons, such as Baker's and Booker's.

The Bourbon that's not just a pretty bottle: Woodford Reserve

Big corporations tend to get knocked regularly (usually for good reasons), but Woodford Reserve is a good example of how big can create something small and beautiful. The giant Brown-Forman Corporation pumped large wodges of cash into restoring the historic Labrot and Graham Distillery and, judging by the quality of this silky-smooth charmer, the effort has been worth it. And yes, the old medicine-bottle packaging is fab.

Titter ye not, it's a serious Bourbon: Knob Creek 9 Years

It may sound like a gimmicky brand (the place does actually exist), but there is no gimmickry inside the bottle. A high proportion of rye in the mix, a hefty dose of alcohol, and a lengthy stay in heavily charred barrels all add up to a seriously full-bodied Bourbon that needs to be drunk sitting down.

The original single-barrel Bourbon: Blanton's Single Barrel

Produced from barrels situated in those parts of the warehouse where ageing conditions are best, this is proof (if you needed it) that single barrel is not just a cynical marketing ploy. Toasty caramel, mint, orange peel, vanilla and spice... it's all in here somewhere. Just sit back and enjoy the warm glow, the smooth glide, and the long, dry finish.

A good aperitif Bourbon: Baker's 7 Years

Like Jim Beam, this uses quite a high percentage of corn – you can smell and taste it clearly – and a deep char on the barrels. It starts all creamy and rich, but ends with the sort of dry, astringent finish that makes it perfect early evening material.

The 'I'll get you a drink' bereavement Bourbon: Joseph Finch 15 Years

Not only is this one of the most soothing drops of spirit I've tasted, it also has a mellow character that gives a whole new meaning to the term 'easy-drinking'. All the comfort flavours are here (vanilla, caramel, cinnamon). Though there's fire in its belly, it's a slow, steady flame rather than a gum-numbing fireball.

The Bourbon to break the Bourbon virgin's cherry: Rowan's Creek

First-timers often find the bite and heavy oak character of Bourbon a bit too much to handle. With neither of these characteristics, Rowan's Creek is so subtle and smooth, even the most whiskey-phobic vodka drinkers would find themselves getting unintentionally hooked.

The whiskey that's not really a Bourbon: Jack Daniel's

It may taste pretty much the same as a Bourbon, but Jack Daniel's (JD to his regulars) can't call itself a Bourbon. This is because it is a Tennessee whiskey, and has one major difference in its production method. Before being transferred to casks, the spirit is filtered through charcoal to take out impurities, which adds a mellow sweetness to the whiskey.

Whisky: with or without ice and an 'e'

Defining it

It's the water of life, the wee dram that you have to nose to know, the collector's Holy Grail, the greatest Scottish export (after golf and Billy Connolly), and the spirit that has as much of a sense of place as wine.

Making it

To make a malt whisky, you'll have to get your hands on the following things: a distillery (the older and remoter, the better), some basic ingredients (water, malted barley and yeast), a warehouse full of second-hand barrels to age the spirit in, and a large amount of patience. Right, now take the malted barley (drying over peat smoke is an optional extra) and mix it with water to make a beer. Distil this twice to create a raw, clear spirit and put this into your barrel of choice – old Bourbon casks are the norm, but you could try anything from ex-wine *barriques* to sherry casks. Leave to simmer gently in peace and quiet for between eight and 30 years, and then, when you are ready (or rather when your accountant says you are ready), take it out, dilute it to an appropriate strength and put it into bottles.

Tasting it

A whisky's aroma and flavour depend on the sort of water used, the type of barley and the way that barley is malted, the method of distillation and the way the spirit is aged. Whisky's greatest selling points are its variety and complexity, and tasting (or rather nosing) whisky is a journey through an amazing landscape of welcoming whiffs and strange scents. Expect to encounter everything from smoke and seaweed to dried fruits and medicine cabinets.

Drinking it

Nosing and sipping are the name of the game here, and you can either drink it neat or with a little spring water. Careful dilution helps release more flavour and helps rein in the alcoholic excesses of cask-strength whiskies. There are some strange people who argue that whisky has been woefully underused in the cocktail arena, but in my opinion, mixing it with something apart from water deserves a long apprenticeship in an isolated peat bog.

Experiencing it

Getting the best out of whisky requires going somewhere with abysmally bad weather, questionable gastronomy and a distinct lack of daylight hours. In short, you've got to visit Scotland.

Speaking it

BLENDED WHISKY Blends are made by mixing different grain and malt whiskies into brands that have a consistent style and flavour.

SINGLE MALT An unblended malt whisky made from a single distillery.

VATTED MALT A blend of malt whiskies from different distilleries.

CASK STRENGTH A whisky that is bottled straight from the cask without being reduced to a lower strength with water.

WOOD FINISHES The use of different types of barrels to add specific character to a malt whisky.

PEAT REEK The pungent smell of peat smoke that can sometimes be found in the nose of a single malt.

Reinventing it

Single malts like Ardbeg might be enjoying cult status in the spirit-drinking world, but Scotch whisky in general is still distinctly lacking in the bar-cred department. Asking for a wee dram or (God forbid) a Whisky Mac in a style bar will get you as much amused attention as a request for a pint of real ale and a glass of fine wine. Instead of reinventing itself, the whisky industry has decided to milk the heritage and rarity angles for all they're worth; their target market remains the mature, 'thinking' drinker rather than the younger crowd that drinks in order not to think.

The classic whisky drink: The Hot Toddy

If you live in the tropics, you can skip this bit, but if you live in a place where cold fronts and low cloud are a daily rather than monthly phenomenon, this recipe will be essential. A good hot toddy will help remove aches and pains, provide internal heat therapy, make a cold seem worthwhile, and give you a good excuse to drink whisky in the morning. Mix a healthy slug of whisky (blends will do) with lemon juice, honey, hot water, cinnamon and cloves.

CHOOSING WHISKY

The everyday drinking whisky: Johnny Walker Red Label

Browse around a duty-free shop or supermarket booze aisle and you can guarantee you'll bump into names like Bell's, Johnny Walker and Famous Grouse. These are the Jacob's Creeks of the whisky world: relatively cheap, heavily marketed products made by blending different components. When they're good, they have just as much complexity and style as a blended wine like Grange, but when they're bad, they're as bland and dull as Gallo White Zinfandel.

The gentle introduction whisky: Auchentoshan

If you are looking for a first rung on the single-malt ladder, the best place to start is in the Lowlands. Most of these single malts tend to be lighter in style than their more northerly friends, and because they use little peat, they are usually more mellow and sometimes slightly sweet.

The baptism-by-fire whisky: Laphroaig

If, on the other hand, you want to ditch the beginners' course and dive straight into the hard stuff, Islay is the place to head. Often heavily peated and influenced by the sea air, these island malts are the Quentin Tarantino productions of the whisky world: loud, intricately plotted adult entertainment with good potential for cult status. Lots of smoke, lots of weed (seaweed), and maybe even some iodine for medicinal purposes.

The cult whisky: Ardbeg

To gain status in the fraternity of cultdom, the single malt in question must have a lot of character, a long and chequered history with possible supply problems and/or threat of closure, a good name and a respectfully low level of marketing. Ardbeg – one of Islay's most extrovert malts – covers all the bases, but with new owners and lots of investment it'll have to be careful it doesn't become too mainstream.

The dead-but-not-buried whisky: Ladyburn

Thanks to the time-lag between a whisky being made and when it is eventually bottled, a distillery can live on in spirit long after it has been relegated to mothball status. William Grant recently released a Ladyburn 1973 cask-strength whisky – despite the fact this lowland distillery closed down over 20 years ago.

The cask-strength whisky: Springbank 1966 Cask Strength

Cask-strength whiskies are stronger but not necessarily better than their standard-strength cousins. Given that you'll probably need to dilute it yourself to make it drinkable, the question 'What is the point of cask strength?' is reasonably valid.

The independent, bottled whisky: Connoisseur's Choice

A number of companies buy stocks of malt whiskies from different distilleries and age and bottle them under their own independent labels. This can be a good source for rarities, but also cheaper versions of distillery-named products.

The barrel-lovers whisky: Glenmorangie Port Wood Finish

An increasing number of distilleries are experimenting with different styles of wood (old barrels once used for sherry, Madeira, port or wine) to add an edge to their whiskies. How much is marketing hype and how much is a quality is debatable, but these 'finishes' are taking whisky flavour in interesting new directions.

The collector's whisky: The Bowmore 1957

The collector's whisky is easy to spot. It usually carries the tag 'limited release', sits in a case that often costs more than its contents, and comes at a price that requires you never to unscrew the top. The Holy Grail of the collector is an old, small-production, cask-strength whisky from a now-defunct distillery, packaged in a case made from the barrels in which it was aged.

The whisky with an 'e': Irish

The Irish don't just spell it differently (whiskey), they make it differently, too. Triple distillation is the norm, and this tends to produce a lighter, smoother style of spirit. Paddy, Bushmills, Jameson, Power's... even the names are more approachable than their often unpronounceable Scottish counterparts.

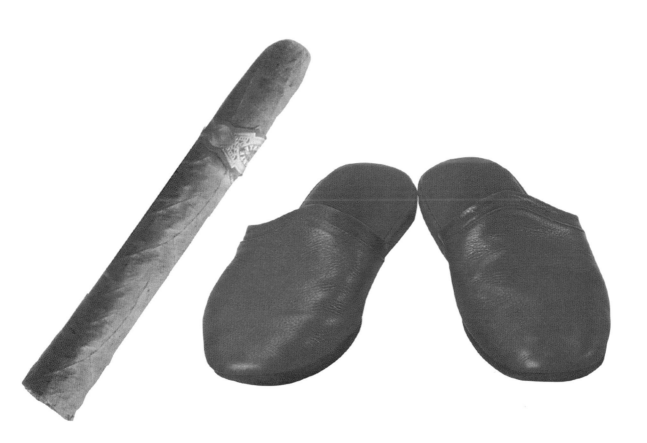

Brandy: from sexy slow-burners to rough Bunsen burners

Defining it

The word 'brandy' – spirit distilled from any fruit, whether grapes, pears, apples or whatever the local DIY distiller can get his or her hands on – covers a multitude of saints and sinners. It can be one of the most sophisticated and memorable drinks on the planet, but also one of the roughest and most forgettable experiences in the book.

Making it

Take your chosen fruit – grapes if you are making Cognac and Armagnac, apples if you are making Calvados – and ferment it into alcohol. If you are using grapes, you want ones that produce relatively neutral flavours but good acidity, and you want your resulting wine to be good quality (distilling concentrates bad things as well as good things). Distil the alcohol to spirit, and then put it into casks to age and mellow out.

Tasting it

If your nose has been lying a little dormant of late, a large inhalation of fine XO Cognac is probably the best wake-up call it will ever get.

As wave after wave of stewed fruits, vanilla, spice, muscovado sugar, nuts, smoke and marzipan wafts up the nostrils, everything (sinuses, brain, eyes) seems to get a good, life-affirming fumigation. And if your insides lack a little warmth, take a good gulp and feel the effects of the best internal central-heating system in the world.

Drinking it

First of all, you don't need a large stately pile, a collection of balloon-shaped glasses and a plum lodged in your mouth to be eligible for Team Brandy. Second, don't be afraid to break convention. Add ice to your Cognac, serve Armagnac chilled if you want, and feel free to mix your brandy with ginger ale, soda water, orange juice or Coke.

Experiencing it

The wide range of styles of brandy means there is no uniform definition of what a good brandy moment is. A cold glass of Pisco Sour high in Chile's Elqui Valley will be very different from the short, sharp shock of a glass of grappa, which in turn will be nothing like a soothing glass of Armagnac drunk late at night in front of an open fire. Brandy can be experienced on the tightest of budgets with the most down-to-earth, humble people or on the most elastic of expense accounts with a bunch of complete bankers.

Speaking it

VS 'Very Special', this is the basic Cognac aged for at least three years.

VSOP 'Very Special Old Pale', this style of Cognac has to be at least four-and-a-half years old.

XO 'Extra Old' should be at least eight years old and can be far older.

CHAMPAGNE COGNAC Refers to the flat chalkland whence the best Cognacs originate and not to a spirit made from the bubbly stuff.

EAU DE VIE Literally 'water of life', this is the generic French term for all brandies.

AGUARDIENTE The spanish word for a high-proof spirit made in a continuous still.

Reinventing it

Back in the days when the smoking jacket was an essential dining accessory and working hours for gentlemen were such that hangovers were workable headaches, brandy sales boomed. Those days are past – drink-driving laws and the health police have been the chief culprits – and this spirit is in the doldrums. But wait, the comeback is afoot. Chilled Cognac shots, sleek, duty-free gifts, cigar-matching brands, single-estate brandies... it's a post-prandial, Jim, but not as we know it.

The classic brandy drink:
The Sidecar

Every cocktail has to have a good (and totally unverifiable) historical anecdote tagged to its creation. The Sidecar story goes like this. American soldiers fighting in France come up with a cocktail based on the local ingredients (Cognac and Cointreau). One particular soldier drinks too much of said concoction and has to be ferried back to barracks in the passenger compartment of his motorbike. *Voilà: le Sidecar est arrivé*. To make one, take a triple measure of Cognac and single measures of Cointreau and lemon juice. Shake with ice and strain into a sugar-rimmed Martini glass.

CHOOSING BRANDY

Cognac: Hennessy, Hine, Rémy Martin, Courvoisier...

The most famous, the most revered, and the most expensive brandy in the world comes from the region centred on the town of Cognac in Southwest France. Cognac is made by (twice) distilling wine made from Ugni Blanc grapes and then ageing it in barrels for a minimum of three years. The style and price of Cognac will depend on where the grapes came from (there are seven appellations of varying quality), the length of time that the spirit is aged, and the reputation (ego) of the producer. Of the cheaper models (look for VS on the label), the brands to target are Hine Signature and Rémy Martin Grand Cru.

Cigar-matching Cognacs: Cohiba Cognac Extra, Davidoff Extra Selection, Hine Cigar Reserve

A quiet day in the marketing department, a long, lazy lunch with a cigar to finish, and a bit of hassle patching a call through to Cuba – this is all it took for a whole new Cognac category to be born. If you are even the least bit cynical of all that food-and-wine-matching tosh, you'll be deeply suspicious of a bunch of expensive Cognacs made to match mouthfuls of smoke. Mind you, that Cohiba stuff is a lovely drop of spirit.

Armagnac: Janneau, Laressingle, Tariquet...

The thinking-person's brandy, the most undervalued spirit in the world, France's best-kept secret – I've heard Armagnac described as all these things and more. Although often bundled together with Cognac, it is a completely different kettle of spirit. Made from different grapes (from very different soils), distilled (only once) in a different type of still, and aged in very different oak, it is lower in alcohol but tends to be richer and more pungent than Cognac. The Armagnac area – located in Gascony to the south of Bordeaux – is divided into three regions, and the best-quality spirits come from Bas-Armagnac and Tenarèze.

Brandy de Jerez: González-Byass, Domecq, Osborne

Although more renowned for its finos and olorosos, the Spanish town of Jerez has a long brandy-making history. Made with hot-climate grapes and the same pyramid-filtering (*solera*) system used for ageing sherry, these brandies are nothing like their more famous French cousins. They are usually darker in colour, softer and mellower in the mouth, and tend to have some of the characteristic oxidative flavours found in sherry.

Grappa: Poli, Zeni, Francoli, Bertagnolli, Nonino

Normally drunk by farmers and manual workers in northern Italy – to fire up their internal central heating and numb them from the next mundane task – grappa has been trying to shake off its rustic image and mingle with the posh Cognac crowd. Prompted by improvements (and rising prices) in Italian wine, distillers have completely changed their attitude to a product that was once treated as a post-harvest afterthought. The locals might be laughing at the ridiculous new packaging, the single-varietal grappas and the optimistic pricing policies, but even they couldn't

deny that this rural spirit now tastes better than ever before.

Fruit brandies: Calvados, Poire William, eaux-de-vie

A variety of fruit-based distillates are made across Europe, and probably the most famous of these is the French apple brandy known as Calvados. Usually made by small, artisan producers, these clear, strongly flavoured spirits are normally served as digestifs.

Pisco: Alto del Carmen, Pisco Control, Capel

South America's gift to the brandy-quaffing gods is Pisco, and the two main producing countries are Chile and Peru. Made by distilling wine produced from aromatic grape varieties such as Muscat and Moscatel, and then ageing it in local beech barrels, the spirit tends to be very fragrant, and the 'aged' versions can be excellent. Mixed with lemon and sugar, it makes one of the most brain-rattlingly good summer cocktails on earth: the Pisco Sour.

Absinthe: the Green Fairy returns

As comebacks go, the return of Absinthe in the 1990s was as surprising as John Travolta's return to the spotlight in *Pulp Fiction*. A drink that was thought to have disappeared along with Van Gogh's ear and a long list of inebriated bohemians suddenly returned to active duty, and became the most fashionable spirit at millennium parties. A spirit once deemed so potent that *renverser ton absinthe* meant 'to kick the bucket' was back on bar lists again – and barely a whimper of protest was heard.

The history of this drink is as colourful as it is long. Although its roots are thought to go back to ancient Greece, when mixtures of wormwood leaves and wine were used to ease rheumatism and menstrual pain, the concoction that became known as 'bottled madness' was created around the time of the French Revolution. A certain Dr Ordinaire fled to Switzerland, where possibly bored – with clean air and mountain views – he created a new drink using wormwood bark, star anise, liquorice, fennel and coriander.

He named it after *Artemisia absinthium,* the botanical name for wormwood.

After Ordinaire died, some time later the recipe was bought by two Frenchmen, and production eventually moved to a distillery in the Jura Mountains. With its strange colour and alleged hallucinogenic properties, it didn't take long for absinthe to become the drink of choice among artists such as Degas, Toulouse-Lautrec and Manet. Some of their best work was said to have been inspired by images and experiences associated with it.

By the 1850s, however, there were growing concerns over the effects of overindulgence, and doctors had even identified a new category of alcoholism called 'absinthism'. Although the symptoms were probably caused by nothing more than a combination of alcohol and syphilis, many believed it was thujone – a chemical found in wormwood – which caused the strange side-effects. Eventually, the drink was banned in France and other countries, and this state of prohibition remains in place today.

Fortunately for modern-day bohemians, no such legislation was ever written for the UK. When someone began importing Hills Absinthe into London bars, there was nothing the authorities could do. What started as a green trickle quickly turned into a high-alcohol flood, and a wide variety of brands is now available. The one that most bartenders swear by is called La Fée, and if you drink enough of it, I guarantee you'll eventually see a strange, white, round vision (otherwise known as the toilet bowl).

Making it

Absinthe – like gin – is basically a flavoured vodka. Instead of botanicals, you macerate oil of wormwood and a variety of herbs and spices in neutral alcohol. These might include fennel, hyssop, cinnamon, lemon balm, star anise and angelica. In Toulouse-Lautrec's time, the green colour would have come purely from the chlorophyll in the wormwood plants, but today, it is boosted with ingredients such as turmeric and indigo.

Drinking it

Because absinthe is very strong and very bitter, the traditional way of drinking it involves a little sweetening and dilution. In the Czech Republic, they take it a step further with a ritual guaranteed to give the wrong impression if performed at the annual family Christmas party.

1 Pour a double shot of absinthe into a short tumbler.
2 Take a teaspoon of sugar and dip it gently into the absinthe so that it becomes soaked with the spirit.
3 Ignite the sugar so that it bubbles and just starts to caramelize.
4 When the flame is out, stir the sugar into the absinthe and finally add ice and a double measure of water.

Can it do strange things to your head?

While it is true that thujone does have a similar structure to the active ingredient in marijuana, there is little scientific evidence that it has a similar effect on the brain. The simple truth is that most absinthe has a very high alcohol level (sometimes up to 70 percent) and if you drink enough of anything this strong, you'll probably start to hallucinate.

Liqueurs: slick, sweet and desperately seeking a spin doctor

Defining them

Liqueurs are sweetened drinks made by mixing or re-distilling base spirit(s) with flavourings and colourings. They are also one of the most common causes of holiday hangovers, a familiar feature in airport duty-free shops around the world, and an important arsenal of flavour for the creative mixologist.

Making them

You name it and there's a fair chance that someone has tried to make a liqueur with it. Sometimes the ingredients and production methods are so simple you could probably make your own DIY version at home; at other times the techniques are so complex and secret that it is almost impossible to replicate the style. The basic idea is as follows. Take a base spirit (usually high-strength, neutral alcohol) and inject some flavour into it by either macerating/infusing your chosen ingredient(s) in it, percolating the spirit through the ingredient(s), or re-distilling the spirit with the ingredient(s). Having done one or a combination of these, you might then like to age the flavoured spirit before sweetening it with sugar syrup. Adding cream is an optional extra.

Tasting them

You can accuse liqueurs of a lot of things, but you can't accuse of them of lacking flavour. Whether it's the zesty, bitter-orange flavour of Cointreau, the intense, blackcurrant character of cassis or the rich, almond notes of Amaretto, these are drinks that have enough personality to change the character of a cocktail with just one small measure.

Drinking them

Apart from the odd exception (did someone mention flaming Sambucas?), liqueurs are made to be sipped and savoured rather than knocked back like some sort of unwanted medicine. With their silky, viscous textures and sweet taste, they make perfect late-night wind-down drinks that are best served on ice. You can dilute them (ouzo with water), use them to add flavours to other drinks (crème de cassis added to Champagne), or mix them with spirits to make great cocktails.

Experiencing them

The good-liqueur experience is a warm, feel-good drinking moment that can be as satisfying and comforting as mother's milk.

The bad-liqueur experience is a nightmare trip through out-of-date, holiday-gift hell with an exit door marked 'guaranteed hangover'.

Speaking them

CORDIAL An old-fashioned American term for liqueurs, now somewhat obsolete.

CRÈME DE... A generic term used for a range of concentrated liqueurs that, despite what the title might suggest, do not contain cream.

DOUBLE LIQUEURS Refers to super-concentrated liqueurs that are made to be diluted.

SURFINES A French term for the strongest and sweetest style of liqueur.

SCHNAPPS A confusing generic term that is often used to describe sweet liqueurs as well as the higher-strength, dry spirits found in Germany.

Reinventing it

Despite what you might think from looking at those sexy Baileys ads, asking for a liqueur in a style bar can be as dangerous as going up to the DJ and asking if he's got anything by the Brotherhood of Man. These drinks still have a major image problem. But there are glimmers of hope. Some liqueurs (most notably Southern Comfort) have managed to reposition themselves and convince everyone that they are light spirits rather than liqueurs, while others have simply latched onto our inability to say no to something sweet and creamy. Meanwhile, thanks to their important supporting roles in cocktails (which are currently riding a very fashionable wave), liqueurs are at least getting more exposure than ever before.

The classic liqueur drink: Christmas Eggnog

Liqueurs might be the most unfashionable bottles in the drinks cabinet, but at the time of year that causes the style police to drop their guard, a sort of homemade liqueur-cum-cocktail makes a brief but extremely popular appearance. Eggnog is an American Christmas tradition, and one glance at the 'how to construct' manual and you'll understand why this is a one-night-a-year affair. You could do the whole 'egg-separating' act, or you could simply mix some Warnink's Advocaat, brandy and cream and sprinkle some nutmeg on top.

CHOOSING LIQUEURS

Cream liqueurs: Baileys, Amarula, Cadbury's Cream...

This category has grown in the slipstream of Baileys, a cream liqueur that was born out of spirit surplus and a mad idea to make a bottled Irish coffee; it has since become the biggest-selling liqueur of them all. While it might not have the cachet and history of other brands, Baileys is an impressive feat of liquid engineering, managing to fuse alcohol and cream without creating a sour, curdled mess. What began as a gentle flow quickly become a dairy deluge as variations on an alcoholic cream theme were launched; even some of the classic liqueur names have tried to jump on the milk cart. Rich, easy to drink and relatively low in alcohol, cream liqueurs are the comfort blankets of the drinks world.

Crème liqueurs: Crème de Cacao, Crème de Cassis...

Not to be confused with their creamy cousins, crème liqueurs tend to be sweeter and more concentrated than other liqueurs, and are usually used as ingredients in cocktails rather than as stand-alone drinks. Two exceptions to this rule are Kahlúa (a blend of cane spirit, coffee and vanilla) and Tia Maria (coffee and spices infused in Jamaican cane spirit), which are often drunk straight on ice. The crème family includes a wide range of fruit-based liqueurs no decent bartender would be without.

Orange liqueurs: Cointreau, Grand Marnier, Mandarine Napoléon...

Oranges have spawned more liqueurs than any other fruit, and if you are looking for the good, the bad and the ugly (as in bright blue) of the liqueur world, this category has them all. This extensive family of sweet, fruity flavour is often lumped under the title Curaçao liqueurs, after the original Dutch liqueurs made from the peel of bitter Curaçao oranges. My top tip is Mandarine Napoléon, a zesty-but-silky liqueur made with Sicilian oranges, various botanicals and Cognac.

Whisk(e)y liqueurs: Drambuie, Southern Comfort, Irish Mist...

This motley crew might all use a similar base spirit, but – thanks to the use of a range of other ingredients – the taste spectrum is wide. The most famous two are Drambuie (the sweet, spicy kick in a Rusty Nail) and Southern Comfort, a peachy concoction that probably has more bar-cred than any other liqueur. The Scots have not been slow to sweeten up their drams, either. While malt-drinking purists might shudder at the prospect of a glass of Stag's Breath or Cock o' the North, these 'whiskies for sweet tooths' taste far better than they sound.

Nutty liqueurs: Amaretto, Malibu, Madrono...

Infusing nuts in spirit is a rural tradition across much of Europe, and if you are more of a nut than a fruit case, you might like to try one of these. Amaretto gets its lovely rich, marzipan flavour from almonds; Madrono has developed a cult following (in Spain) for its walnut-inspired character; and Malibu keeps the clichéd advertisement alive with its 'totally tropical' coconut taste.

Divine liqueurs: Chartreuse, Bénédictine....

If anyone should be credited with putting liqueurs on the map, it is the monks who spent many silent hours creating health-giving elixirs in the Middle Ages. Today, some of the best (and most secretive) liqueur-making still goes on in monasteries, with possibly the most famous and revered being Chartreuse. Over a hundred different ingredients are used to make this very strong and strongly flavoured liqueur that comes in green and yellow versions. And no, it doesn't make you wake up with a strange round bald patch.

The 'I brought it back from holiday' liqueurs: Sambuca, Izarra...

One of the stranger habits of suitcase-carrying *Homo sapiens* is the need to bring back a liquid memento from holiday. And what seemed such a good idea in the airport duty-free shop invariably comes back to haunt you at about 3AM a year later, when you scramble through your cupboards to find something to drink.

Cocktails, but no umbrellas, please

Unless you've been a teetotal hermit for the last decade, you can't fail to have noticed that cocktails have changed into new clothes. From a dire period where Sex on the Beach, Zombies and Brain Haemorrhages were as sophisticated as it got, we've emerged into a golden age of experimentation, invention and – most importantly of all – decent-tasting drinks. Spirits have become the height of fashion, mixology has become the new rock 'n' roll, and bartenders have moved from wage-slaving heroes of the mixing desk to salary-earning stars with big profiles and often even bigger egos.

But are the cocktails of today better than those made by the maestros of the jazz age? To a large extent, the answer has to be yes, because, regardless of different skill levels, there is absolutely no doubt that the quality and range of ingredients have improved dramatically. Today's cocktail-maker has an enviable portfolio of premium spirits and ingredients such as fresh, exotic juices and pulps. Net result? Classic cocktails are being reinvented, undiscovered classics are being unearthed, and lists of new classics are being created.

Obviously, it's not all good news. As with any period of creativity, there are times when things slip from the sublime to the ridiculous, then way on down to the plain absurd. The good old Martini has been tweaked and nudged in so many directions (I've even seen slices of rare beef being slipped into the glass) that we've lost sight of how good the original was. Somewhere in the rush to make the next best thing, cocktail barmen have forgotten that simplicity is the essence of a great cocktail. Just as too many cooks can spoil the broth, so, too, can too many ingredients ruin the bevvy.

The same rule is even more relevant for the amateur DIY mixer. All the cocktails in this book have been designed with simple assembly in mind. There are no special syrups included in the recipes, no rare cult spirits that can be found only in the Bangkok duty-free shop, no bottle-juggling tricks to be performed and no complicated instructions to be followed. If you understand how to write a cheque, you can definitely make any one of these drinks.

The essential cocktail kit

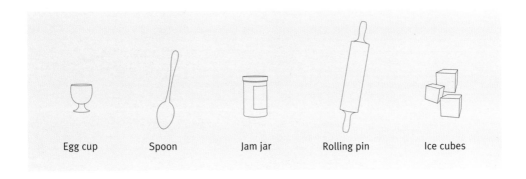

Egg cup Spoon Jam jar Rolling pin Ice cubes

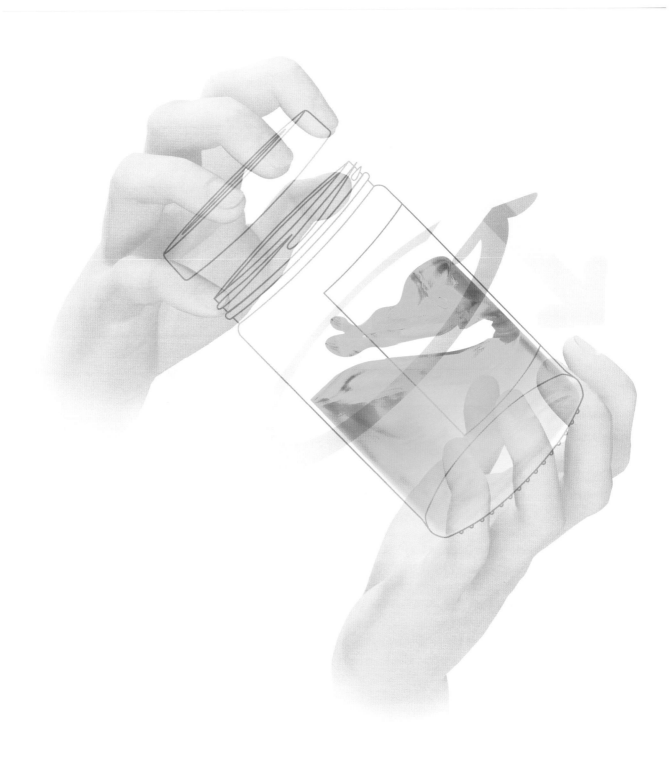

Kick-ass cocktails

The first cocktail of the night is an important one. This is a drink that should rattle the senses, crank up the tempo and set the tone for whatever happens in the next few hours. These are the sort of drinks that can change the mood of a party, wake up even the most jet-lagged traveller and change plans of 'just one quick drink' into an impromptu all-nighter.

CAIPIRINHA

GLASS:	Short and stubby

INGREDIENTS: Double measure Cachaça (Brazilian rum)   1 lime / 2 brown sugar cubes / Crushed ice

WHAT YOU DO: Cut the lime into eighth segments, squeeze the pieces into the glass and (with the sugar) crush them with a pestle to get the zest and oils out of the skin. You could use any type of sugar, but a coarse version will help grind the skins. If you don't have a pestle, just use anything blunt and wooden (the handle of a hammer will do). Then fill up the glass with crushed ice and Cachaça and serve with a straw.

PISCO SOUR

GLASS: Short and stubby

INGREDIENTS: 1 bottle of Pisco / Lemons and limes   Sugar / Ice

WHAT YOU DO: It's easier to make Pisco Sours for a few people than for one. Pour one bottle of Pisco (a type of brandy made in Chile and Peru) into a big jug. Add a full mug of mixed lemon and lime juice, six tablespoons of sugar, and ice. Stir and serve. If you have a container that allows you to shake everything, even better, but stirring in a bowl is fine. Using a cocktail shaker, the normal ratio is three parts Pisco to one part lemon/lime juice.

COOL-HAND LUKE

GLASS: Tall and thin

INGREDIENTS: 1 lime / 4 drops Angostura bitters   2 tsps dark-brown sugar / Double measure dark rum / Crushed ice

WHAT YOU DO: Cut the lime into eight segments. Put the lime, sugar and bitters in the glass and mix well. Add the rum and crushed ice and serve with a straw.

THE MINI-ME MARGARITA

GLASS: Shot glass

INGREDIENTS: Single measure Tequila   Juice of ½ a lime

1 dash Cointreau   Ice

WHAT YOU DO: Put all the ingredients into a mixer, shake, and strain into a shot glass. When making these, it's best to mix up enough for a few people. If you make it for one, you'll invariably get too much ice to too little liquid and the drink will seem dilute.

METROPOLIS

GLASS: Martini (from freezer)

INGREDIENTS: Double measure Absolut Mandrin   1 dash Mandarine Napoléon

Single measure lemon juice   1 dash sugar syrup

WHAT YOU DO: Pour all the ingredients into a cocktail shaker with some cubes of ice. Shake vigorously, then strain into the glass. Finish off by spraying the zest from some orange skin onto the top of the cocktail.

MIMOSA FRAPPÉ

GLASS: Tall and thin

INGREDIENTS: 3 slices of orange (including rind)   Single measure lemon juice

1 tsp dark-brown sugar   Double measure dark rum

1 dash Cointreau   Champagne

WHAT YOU DO: Squeeze the orange into the glass, then put the skins in the glass and mix around with the sugar (*à la* Caipirinha). Add the lemon juice, Cointreau and rum. Top up with crushed ice and float some Champagne over the lot.

DIY TIP 1 – SUGAR SYRUP

One of the essential ingredients for cocktails is sugar syrup. You can buy it quite easily, but making your own is simple and less expensive. Just pour 500g (1 lb 2oz) of white sugar into 250ml (8 fl oz) of water and heat and stir until all the sugar is dissolved. Cool and store in a bottle in the fridge.

Wind-down cocktails

Feeling in need of a little liquid therapy? Looking for a soothing drink to help you warm up and chill out at the same time? Well, here are some cocktails for the times you don't give a monkey's about fashion and couldn't give a fig about post-prandial protocol. All are best drunk while wearing slippers and one of those fluffy white bathrobes you nicked from that five-star hotel.

HOT TODDY

GLASS:	A heatproof glass or a mug
INGREDIENTS:	Double measure whisky (blended) 1 cinnamon stick
	Juice 1 lemon 4 or 5 whole cloves
	2 heaped tsps honey Hot water
WHAT YOU DO:	Spike the cloves into a thick slice of lemon so that they don't float around and end up being swallowed. Pour all the other ingredients into the glass, leaving the honey until last (it will come off the spoon more easily if you stir it into the hot liquid). The cinnamon stick can just sit and soak in the glass.

BRANDY BLAZER

GLASS:	Cognac 'balloon' glass
INGREDIENTS:	Double measure best Cognac 1 brown sugar cube
	Long strip orange zest
WHAT YOU DO:	Heat the Cognac by putting the bottle into an ice bucket of hot water (wrap the bottle in a plastic bag if you don't want the label to come off). Cut off a piece of orange zest with a potato peeler and put it into the glass along with the sugar cube. Once the Cognac is warm, pour it into the glass and light it. Let it burn for 10 to 15 seconds and then extinguish by putting a damp tea towel on top of the glass. This is a great one to make if you are staying with your parents: they're bound to have a bottle of Cognac and the right type of glass.

ORANGE DAIQUIRI

GLASS:	Martini glass (from freezer)
INGREDIENTS:	Double measure good golden rum Splash of fresh orange juice
	Single measure lime juice 2 tsps sugar syrup

WHAT YOU DO: Pour all ingredients into a cocktail shaker with some ice. Shake vigorously and strain into a frozen glass. Finish off by spraying the oil from some orange zest on top.

WHITE RUSSIAN

GLASS: Short and stubby

INGREDIENTS: Double measure vodka   Single measure Kahlúa

Single measure single cream

WHAT YOU DO: Pour the vodka and the Kahlúa into a cocktail shaker with some ice. Shake well, then strain into a glass filled with ice. Finally, pour in the cream over the back of a spoon.

SOHO BULLDOG

GLASS: Tall and thin

INGREDIENTS: Single measure vodka   Single measure Kahlúa

Single measure Baileys   Single measure fresh cream

Coca-Cola

WHAT YOU DO: Pour all the ingredients (except the Coke) into a glass filled with some roughly crushed ice. Stir well and add a splash of Coke. It might sound like a horrible mixture, but believe me: this tastes great.

TREACLE

GLASS: Short and stubby

INGREDIENTS: Double measure dark rum   1 dash sugar syrup

4 drops Angostura bitters   Splash of apple juice

WHAT YOU DO: Pour one shot of the rum into a glass with a couple of ice-cubes. Add the bitters and syrup and stir thoroughly. Add the rest of the rum and a bit more ice and stir some more. Add a splash of apple juice, fill up with ice and spray oil from some lemon zest on top of the drink.

DIY TIP 2 – CRUSHED ICE

If you don't have a blender or one of those nice little ice-crushers, just put some ice-cubes in a clean tea towel and hammer them with a rolling pin.

Healthy cocktails

If you were to believe all the current medical reports on the benefits of moderate alcohol consumption, you'd probably argue that all cocktails are healthy in some way. But for those who really want to give their livers a complete break, here are some non-alcoholic drinks that are guaranteed to leave you bright-eyed rather than bleary. A blender is essential here.

THE BIG C

GLASS: Tall and thin

INGREDIENTS: 1 fresh, ripe guava · A few raspberries
1 ripe peach · Honey, to taste
2 slices fresh ginger

WHAT YOU DO: This thick-textured, spicy, tropical punch makes great cold-prevention material: guavas contain five times more vitamin C than oranges. Put all the ingredients into a blender, making sure you crush the fresh ginger (a couple of slices will do) before putting it in. Blend for 30 seconds, then pour into the glass.

HONEY RIDES

GLASS: Tall and thin

INGREDIENTS: ½ a banana · ½ a passion-fruit
Juice of 1 orange · Dollop of natural yoghurt
Honey, to taste

WHAT YOU DO: Put everything into a blender with some crushed ice, adding honey according to taste. The alcoholic version of this is made with a couple of shots of rum, and I don't care what the medical experts say – I'm convinced it's just as healthy for you.

CHESKA

GLASS: Tall and thin

INGREDIENTS: ½ a pear · 5 fresh raspberries
½ a passion-fruit · ½ a glass fresh apple juice
2 tsps soft, dark-brown sugar

WHAT YOU DO: Put everything into a blender (take the core out of the pear first, though), add some crushed ice and blend for about 30 seconds.

VIRGIN MARY

GLASS: Tall and thin

INGREDIENTS: Tomato juice — 1 tsp horseradish sauce
4 dashes Worcestershire sauce — Squeeze of fresh lemon juice
3 drops Tabasco sauce — 1 celery stick (optional)
Ground black pepper

WHAT YOU DO: Put everything into a cocktail shaker with some ice. Shake and pour into a tall, ice-filled glass. If you're hungover and need assistance, add a good shot of vodka.

PASSIONART

GLASS: Tall and thin

INGREDIENTS: ¹/₂ a passion-fruitFresh apple juice
2 teaspoons sugar syrup — Freshly squeezed orange juice
Puréed strawberries

WHAT YOU DO: Shake all the ingredients, together with some ice, in a cocktail shaker, making sure the ratio of orange to apple juice is 2:1. You needn't blend the strawberries; just mush a few ripe ones with the back of a spoon. Pour into an ice-filled glass.

DETOX DECAMERON

GLASS: Tall and thin

INGREDIENTS: ¹/₄ papaya (deseeded, skinned) — Juice of 1 lime
¹/₂ a glass of apple juice — Dash coconut cream

WHAT YOU DO: Put everything into a blender, add some crushed ice and blend for about 30 seconds. Again, you can add rum to this to give it a kick.

DIY TIP 3 – COCKTAIL SHAKER

If you don't have a cocktail shaker, use a large jam jar (emptied and cleaned, of course) and two lids. Puncture one lid with holes and use this to strain your cocktail into the glass.

DIY TIP 4 – BLENDERS

With a blender, the simplest non-alcoholic drinks to make are smoothies. The basic ingredients are fruit, honey and yoghurt (use frozen yoghurt to avoid crushing ice). Invent your own recipes according to what's lying around in the kitchen.

Seductive or retro cocktails

Okay, you've set the scene for one of those Barry White moments. You've flicked the dimmer switch down to 'Is that you over there?' level, piled all your rubbish in the nearest available closet, and hidden all embarrassing pictures, CDs and cuddly toys. Now all you need to do is prepare a cocktail guaranteed to taste so sexy that even when your guest spots the large tube of athlete's foot cream in the bathroom, he or she still won't run out the door screaming.

FRENCH 75

GLASS:	Champagne flute
INGREDIENTS:	Double measure gin 1 dash sugar syrup
	Squeeze of lemon juice Champagne or sparkling wine
WHAT YOU DO:	Shake the gin, lemon juice and sugar with ice and strain into a Champagne flute. Top with Champagne, then drop a long curl of lemon zest into the glass. If you use sparkling wine, make sure it is a good one; with cheap ones, the bubbles don't last long.

CLASSIC CHAMPAGNE COCKTAIL

GLASS:	Champagne flute
INGREDIENTS:	Single measure brandy 2–3 drops Angostura bitters
	1 white sugar cube Champagne
WHAT YOU DO:	Moisten the sugar cube with the bitters and drop it into the Champagne flute. Add the brandy first, then top up the glass with Champagne.

ABSOLUTE PASSION

GLASS:	Martini (from freezer)
INGREDIENTS:	Double measure vodka $\frac{1}{2}$ a passion-fruit
	1 tbsp strawberry purée 2 tsps sugar syrup
WHAT YOU DO:	Put everything into a shaker along with some ice (just mash a few ripe strawberries to make a purée) and shake vigorously. Pour, and drop in one strawberry as a garnish.

CREAMISSIMO

GLASS:	Tall and thin
INGREDIENTS:	Single measure Baileys · 1 banana
	Single measure Kahlúa · Double measure single cream
WHAT YOU DO:	Blend everything, along with some crushed ice, for 30 seconds, pour and serve.

BRANDY ALEXANDER

GLASS:	Martini glass (from freezer)
INGREDIENTS:	Double measure Cognac · Single measure white crème de cacao
	Ground nutmeg · Single measure fresh cream
WHAT YOU DO:	Another classic cocktail with the sexiest of textures. Put everything except the nutmeg into a cocktail shaker along with some ice. Shake, pour and finish off by sprinkling some nutmeg on top.

APHEXION

GLASS:	Tall and thin
INGREDIENTS:	Double measure Bourbon · 3 brown sugar cubes
	4 strawberries · Splash of orange juice
	½ a passion-fruit · Small wedge of fresh melon (remove skin)
WHAT YOU DO:	The various fruit flavours combine brilliantly here. Put everything into a blender along with some crushed ice. Blend, pour and serve.

DIY TIP 5 – ICE COOL

Because alcohol has a lower freezing point than water, you can keep your bottles of vodka and gin in the freezer without fear of broken bottles. Keeping a bottle of each of these next to the ice means that at the very least, you can serve up an excellent Martini at a minute's notice.

DIY TIP 6 – GARNISH

Life is too short to stress about garnishes, but drinks do look pretty naked without something to finish them off. Keep limes (more versatile than lemons) and mint around at all times, and you can at least make two drinks (Mojitos and Caipirinhas) where the ingredients are the garnish.

Beer cocktails

With bartenders running out of ways to squeeze the Martini into new-flavoured clothes, and under pressure to make the next bar list more innovative than the last, it is only a matter of time before mixologists bring beer into the cocktail arena.

You might think the idea both repugnant and extremely unlikely, but the fact is that people have been mixing things with their beer for years. In Germany, Berliner *Weissbier* (wheat beer) has often been laced with Schnapps, and Berlin-based brewery Kindl has even published a book on mixed drinks using *Weissbier* as a base, offering suggestions such as wheat beer with orange juice. Over in Canada, braver souls have soothed sore heads with a Calgary Red Iron: an avoidable mix of lager, tomato juice and raw egg.

Here in Britain, diluting beer has always been viewed with the utmost disrespect. Whatever their merits in terms of refreshment, the Shandy and the Lager Top are drinks to be ordered in whispers rather than shouts. Perhaps the closest we've come to a successful beer cocktail is the Black Velvet (Champagne and Guinness), but understandably, the Champenois have made concerted efforts to ensure that it never leaves the confines of fading oyster bars.

More recently, a bunch of Belgian exiles have injected some much-needed inspiration into this neglected area of the bar list. It all started a few years ago with the launch of the Belgo 'beer and mussels' chain in London, and the introduction of an off-the-cuff creation called the Schnoegaarden (a shot of fruit genever with Hoegaarden beer). Not only did the drink rapidly achieve cult status, but so did the miniature Hoegaarden glasses they served it in.

In essence, the drink was no more than a glorified version of the Depth Charge (a pint of beer with a full shot glass of your favourite spirit dropped inside). Like its cruder predecessor, the Schnoegaarden's kick was extremely potent. After one or two of these, even Plastic Bertrand started to sound okay. Since this early trial, the boys at Belgo have taken their beer cocktail range to more refined heights. Their Monk's Head brings together the famous fruit beer Bellevue Kriek with Mandarine Napoléon liqueur, Schnapps and orange juice, while the Peach Paradise (peach beer with peach Schnapps, genever and Mandarine Napoléon) is an absolute summer classic.

Will these drinks ever take off in other bars? They might not get much support from CAMRA or the Guild of Bartenders, but I believe this new movement could be a saviour in these times of lager floods and flavourless nitro-keg brews. So say it loud, say it proud: 'Shandy with a twist, please, barman!'

The Shandy

The Shandy (or Panaché as the French call it) is a highly underrated drink and one that is usually doomed to a fate of wishy-washy lager and cheap, sickly lemonade. Make it with Hoegaarden and homemade lemonade.

The Lager Top

Just as the spritzer was a two-fingered salute to the poor quality of pub wine, the Lager Top (lager and lime cordial) is essentially a vote of no confidence in cheap, flavourless lager.

The Snake Bite

This mixture of lager (or Guinness) and cider is a favourite of students and masochistic drinkers. The bite comes at about 3AM.

The Shank

Anyone who takes the long route around a golf course will appreciate the restorative properties of a good Shank. Take some ginger beer and add a dash of grapefruit juice, some lemonade and a few drops of Angostura bitters.

And the beer cocktails you might want to avoid...

- Black & Tan (Guinness and bitter)
- Black Russian (Guinness and vodka)
- Dog's Nose (bitter and gin)
- Dragon's Blood (barley wine and rum)
- Bitter & Black (a pint of bitter with a few squirts of blackcurrant)

Beer: desperately seeking respect

Okay, I want you to stop for a second and think how many different wines you've tried in your life. Fifty? A hundred? Most of you will have given up trying to remember them all and I bet even the most conservative of cork-removers will have reached triple figures within a few of years of starting their wine journey.

Now try the same thing with beer. Let's see, you've probably had a few different lagers, a handful of ales, the odd stout every now and again, and don't forget the fruit beer you tried at that Belgian restaurant last month. My guess is that, even with a bit of artistic licence, the number will probably be somewhere in the teens and definitely way behind the wine figure. Agreed, in numerical terms there are probably more wines out there than beers, but that doesn't offer a good enough excuse for our lack of adventure and curiosity in beer-drinking. It also doesn't explain why we often say, 'I'll have a beer' but rarely treat wine with the same generic disdain.

Despite the big overlap between beer- and wine-drinkers, the two continue to look at each other from opposite ends of the bar. Beer is associated with volume, gulping and refreshment; wine is supposedly all about quality, sipping and taste. Beer mixes with conversation (wine with food), fills the stomach (wine occupies the mind), wears blue-collar overalls (wine still slips into posh togs), and causes satisfied burps while wine triggers its own strange, convoluted language. The two also face very different challenges in their quest for more drinkers. While wine has tried to escape its élitist trappings and brand itself as a mass-market product, beer has sought to break free from its working-class associations and branded homogeneity to show that it is just as varied, just as sexy and just as sophisticated as wine.

Its reputation has been tarnished by the loud, often tasteless antics of its lagery sons and nitrogen-injected cousins, but there are now signs that the rest of the family is starting to make an impression. Thirst-quenching wheat beers, flavour-packed fruit beers, single-variety hop beers, microbrews, IPAs, stouts, Lambics, seasonal beers... try a few of these and you'll never go back to asking for 'a beer' again.

What's in beer?

This is the bit where I bombard you with technical jargon and words that sound more like plumbing accessories than drink vocabulary. Well, actually, on second thoughts, I think we'll ditch the gobbledegook and stick with the basics; something tells me that knowledge of decoction and units of bitterness is not exactly vital for furthering your drinking pleasure. All you really need to know is that beer, whether ale or lager, is made from the same four basic ingredients: malt, water, yeast and hops. The exact style of beer will depend on the characteristics of each of these elements and the way in which the brewer uses them.

MALT

To make an alcoholic drink, you need something with fermentable sugar in it, and for beer-makers that material is malt. First, you choose a cereal – barley, wheat, rye or oats – then you soak the grains in water and allow them to germinate. After about a week, dry them before they start to eat up their own sugar. *Et voilà*! You have malt.

Obviously, if it were as simple as that, the entire beer family would happily fit inside a Morris Minor. But because brewers use different grains (or combinations of) and different types of malt (lightly roasted, pale malts for lighter beers and dark, well-roasted malts for darker beers), you need something more in the range of a fleet of limos to be able to contain all the various permutations.

WATER

A pint of crunchy grains wouldn't be very thirst-quenching, so the next ingredient needs to provide the liquid base. That base is water (called 'liquor' in brewer-speak), and being such a major component in the end product, its character can obviously have a big impact on the final flavour.

Travel around the country you live in and you'll notice – if not by taste, then by the length of time it takes to wash soap off your face – that water varies widely from place to place. Some waters can be soft and alkaline while others are hard and full of minerals, and different brewers will use one or the other depending on what sort of beer they are making.

These days, technology is such that you can replicate a water style from anywhere around the world. This allows big brewing companies to make the same beer in different countries and still get each batch to taste the same.

YEAST

So now you've got a pint of barley-flavoured water, which, admittedly, tastes better than the mouthful of dry grains, but still has something lacking. The missing link is alcohol, and to make it, you need yeast.

Like winemakers, brewers are very fussy about the yeast they use because they know how influential these micro-organisms are in creating a house style. The injection of yeast is the point at which the beer family splits off into lagers and ales. To make an ale, you use a yeast that works near the surface (top-fermenting yeast), and to make a lager you need one that sinks to the bottom (bottom-fermenting yeast) and performs at colder temperatures. A few brewers still use wild rather than cultured yeast, and the resulting beer (known as Lambic beer) has a very distinctive, almost winey flavour.

HOPS AND OTHER FLAVOURINGS

By now, your pint is beginning to resemble beer, but there is one last item you need to help lift it from alcoholic grain-water to something that smells, tastes and feels like the real thing. The fourth and final ingredient is hops, a relation of both the nettle and cannabis plants that is used to add aromatics, bitterness and tannin to a beer.

Due to the strange belief in marketing circles that drinkers prefer beer with as little flavour and bitterness as possible, the use of hops has diminished over the years, but the recent success of single-variety hop beers (think Fuggles instead of Chardonnay) could signal a return to hoppier times. Other flavourings – such as fruit and spices – can also be used to make a variety of specialist beers.

Lager: the great Golden Tsunami

Just as there aren't many parts of the globe that haven't been touched by mobile phones and MTV, there aren't many places where you can't get a cold bottle of lager. Whether you're stuck on a mountain pass in Bolivia or sitting on a Pacific island, you can be fairly sure that the traveller's friend – the international currency of refreshment – will not be far away. Little did those Bavarians realize, when they began storing ('lagering') their beer in icy caves over winter, that one day their unintentional brewing breakthrough would become one of the most commercially successful drinks ever created. For lager is a drink that has crossed more cultural boundaries than the Pope-mobile and quenched more thirst than just about any other alcoholic beverage.

Lager is the drink we resort to when we don't trust the water in a foreign country, the chilly lubrication that helps extinguish the fires of a hot curry, and the cool refreshment we prefer to swig straight from the bottle rather than sip from the glass. Lager is the reason we all spend so much time queueing for the toilet at parties, why American Goliaths have fought courtroom battles with Czech Davids, and why so many ales have disappeared to the Great Booze Cabinet in the sky.

Lager language
Today, its popularity is such that lager has spawned its own lime-laced cocktail (the Lager Top), social group (the Lager Lout), vocabulary ('to get lagered') and art (London's Tate Modern art gallery recently launched its own lager).

I have even heard of lager being used as an economic indicator. 'When the brewery finally closes down, you know a country has slipped from "underdeveloped" to "send for the World Bank" status' was one journalist's assessment after lager production briefly dribbled to a halt in a certain war-torn West African country.

So how did this fizzy, golden beer become such a huge phenomenon?

Back in 1959, lager accounted for only a measly two percent of the British beer market, yet by the turn of the millennium that figure had hit 60 percent, and it is still rising today.

Carling now sells over a billion pints of lager every year in the UK, and they say a pint of Stella Artois is drunk every 19 seconds. It's not so much a golden shower as a golden downpour.

Cold front on the move

You could argue that global warming is making us thirstier for lager, but its success comes down to more than just ozone-layer depletion. Availability is certainly a major factor. As soon as cultured yeast and refrigeration technology arrived, lager was released from its central European stronghold and allowed to spread to any place that had the will and means to build a brewery, the raw materials (water, malted grain, yeast and hops) and a thirsty audience.

Then – in Britain, at any rate – cheap foreign travel arrived. All those millions of package-holiday-makers, who had got hooked on San Miguels and Peronis for two weeks, returned home with a taste for the cold, fizzy stuff and a weakened allegiance to the ale cause.

A decade later, we saw the advent of 'designer' brands such as Sapporo, and suddenly 'badge-drinking' was born: bottles of lager became essential accessories for the label-wearing crowd. The fact that all these marketing-driven products tasted exactly the same appeared to matter very little to a generation looking for a cold, alcoholic hit with as little flavour as possible.

Today, new lager names seem to crop up as quickly as John Galliano hairstyles, and there has even been talk of attempts to make a 'Frankenstein lager', which uses genetically modified yeast to ensure a longer-lasting head.

If and when they do eventually find water on Mars, you can bet one of the first things they'll do is make plans to produce the first Red Planet Lager.

Lagered beers and beers called lager

Even though some drinkers don't actually believe lager is a beer, it should come as no surprise that the aim of the lager brewer is no different from that of his ale counterpart: to take malt, water, hops and yeast and turn it into a refreshing alcoholic beverage.

Yet anyone who has stood a pint of ale and lager side by side will quickly deduce that something slightly different goes on in the lager-making factory, something that turns those four ingredients into something golden, crisp and refreshing rather than flat, fruity and flavoursome. To understand the how and why behind this divergence in styles, we need to reverse a few hundred years to a time before crisps, jukeboxes, and – most importantly – refrigerators.

Birth in Bavaria

The story of lager begins in Germany some time around the 15th century. A bunch of Bavarians decided that the only way their beer would survive storage over the hot summers was if they took it up into the hills and kept it in cool, ice-filled caves. When they returned

a few months later to check up on their liquid nest egg, they found that something strange had happened. Thanks to the effects of cold storage ('lagering'), the beer didn't just taste good, it tasted better than it had when they'd left it.

Now, if at this early stage someone had foreseen where lager would eventually go, they would have immediately slapped a patent on the name (or at least tried to set down some basic rules on how a lager must be made). But because these new lagered beers hadn't exactly shaken up the German beer scene – people still preferred to drink the top-fermented brews – none of the early lager pioneers bothered to protect what they had created. Big mistake, guys, big mistake.

Anyway, things kind of bumbled along until two major technological breakthroughs changed the way the world viewed the amber nectar. First of all, someone developed ice-making machines, which immediately released lager production from the whole cave routine and allowed cold-fermentation techniques to be used in summer as well as winter. Secondly, a scientist working for the Carlsberg laboratories in Denmark managed to isolate the first pure lager yeast culture, allowing brewers to have far greater control over what had previously been a pretty erratic fermentation process. Suddenly, beer-makers everywhere started to see dollar signs.

Ice is nice, but...

Here was a refreshing style of beer that was now far easier to make. Thanks to the fact that it was filtered and stabilized in the brewery, it had also become a beer that could leave the brewery gates with a taste guarantee. The only problem (and it was a big problem) was this whole lagering procedure.

Apart from the fact that refrigeration was costly, most brewers (or rather brewers' accountants) didn't like the idea of having their assets sitting around for up to three months earning nothing. You could say that it was at this point that lager lost its soul.

While there were (and are) strict laws in Germany that governed the ingredients used for making beer, lager-makers in other parts of the world were free to use different grains and additives to help make larger volumes of beer at cheaper prices. In the US, for example, the availability of enzyme-rich barley allowed brewers to use cheaper cereals such as rice and corn; the result was a beer that looked like lager but tasted nothing like those original Bavarian models.

Lagering times were also cut drastically from three months to three weeks, and in the quest to make the perfect 'session' lager (lager that could be drunk in large volumes), brewers cut back on the flavour, reduced the bitterness and lowered the alcohol. The result was a sea of bland lager that provided cold refreshment but little in the way of a taste experience.

Today, there are still plenty of brewers (both in and outside Germany) who adhere to the traditional lagering techniques, but the term 'lager' has become one of the most abused and misused terms in the beer dictionary.

Bud wars: the little details matter

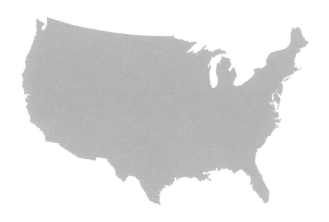

CZECH
REPUBLIC

Budweiser vs Budvar

A TALE OF TWO BUDWEISERS

In the battle for world lager domination, there have inevitably been some international clashes. One particular confrontation has been fizzing gently for decades. On one side of the courtroom sits the world's largest brewer, Anheuser-Busch, and on the other a far smaller, state-controlled Czech brewery called Budweiser Budvar.

Both make a beer called Budweiser, and both believe firmly in their right to use this famous name. The American giant claims that its Budweiser is the original because Adolphus Busch launched it in St Louis, Missouri, at least 16 years before the Budweiser Budvar brewery was established. The Czechs, on the other hand, argue that not only have Budweiser beers been made in their country for centuries, but also that true Budweiser-style beers must come from the town of Ceské Budejovice.

Anyone who has tasted the two side by side will immediately see that, while they might share the same name, the two brewers definitely do not share the same style of beer. One is a very pale, sweetish lager that appears to have very little flavour and is best served extremely cold; the other is a golden (also slightly sweet) lager that has a discernible malt-hop flavour and a long, bitter-edged finish. Unfortunately courtrooms rarely conduct tastings as part of their assessment of evidence, and with so much (profit) at stake, the legal dispute continues to rumble on.

At the moment, the UK is the only country where both beers can use the Budweiser name. In some 33 European countries, the Czechs have the rights to the name and American Budweiser must be sold under the title 'Bud' or 'Anheuser-Busch B'. However, in Spain, Portugal, Denmark, Sweden and Finland, American Budweiser has the right of way and the Czechs must sell their beer as 'Budejovicky Budvar'.

With almost unlimited financial resources, Anheuser-Busch can afford to keep paying its lawyers for as long as it takes, so this David vs Goliath battle is set to run and run. Attempts by the Americans to solve the problem by simply getting out the chequebook and buying this annoying little thorn have so far been met with stern Czech resistance.

Budweiser Budvar

ONCE REFERRED TO AS The Beer of Kings.
MADE IN The town of Ceské Budejovice in the Czech Republic.
PRODUCTION Around 700,000 barrels a year.
AVAILABILITY 58 countries.
HISTORY Established in 1895, 600 years after the first Budweiser beer was brewed in Budweis.
HOW IT IS MADE It is an all-malt beer made with Moravian malt, Saaz hops and soft water from the brewery's own wells. After primary fermentation, the beer is lagered for between 60 and 90 days.
THEY SAY Budweiser Budvar is a typical Budweiser beer characterized by its slightly sweet, delicate and delicious taste, with a pleasant aroma of hops and slight bitterness.
I SAY Sounds about right.
DID YOU KNOW The Czechs are the world's biggest beer guzzlers consuming an average 162 litres per head every year.

Budweiser

ONCE REFERRED TO AS The King of Beers.
MADE IN The US, but also in 11 different countries under the supervision of parent company Anheuser-Busch. The latter was the first US brewer to control a majority interest in a Chinese brewery.
PRODUCTION Over 40 million barrels a year.
AVAILABILITY 80 countries.
HISTORY A guy called Adolphus Busch travelled around central Europe in the late 1860s, looking for a beer style he could make in America. He found what he liked in Bohemia, and returned to launch his version of a Budweis-style beer in 1876. Good marketing, the arrival of refrigerated transport, and the rest is history.
HOW IT IS MADE With a high proportion of rice in the grain mix and a maximum of only a month of lagering time.
THEY SAY Refreshingly different from local brands with its clean, crisp taste and high drinkability.
I SAY It's lager, Jim, but not as we know it.
DID YOU KNOW After Budweiser, the second-biggest-selling beer in the world is Bud Light.

Lager styles

Thanks (or no thanks) to the global success of a certain golden, fizzy, bland beverage, most people have grown to believe that there is only one style of lager: the golden, fizzy, bland one. Ask someone to name three different lager styles and the answer will probably revolve around price (cheap or expensive), alcohol (weak or strong) and whether it has a squirt of lime in it or not.

In fact, there are many different styles, colours and strengths of beer sitting under the lager umbrella. In some cases they bear absolutely no resemblance to the amber-nectar stereotype. Here are some of the lagers you might come across on a round-the-world beer tour.

DARK LAGERS

Travel around the back roads of Germany and you are sure to come across a dark beer called Dunkel. This is the original style of lager – before it headed into new, golden pastures – and as well as looking nothing like a conventional model, it tastes nothing like it, either. Dunkel still has the refreshing cleanness of a lager but tends to be more aromatic. The use of darker malts gives it

some lovely spicy, nutty flavours. Dark lagers can also be found in the Czech Republic and the US.

RED LAGERS

Reddish-coloured lagers originated in Austria, but you can find versions of them from Mexico to Scandinavia. Usually referred to as Vienna-style lagers, these beers have pronounced malty flavours and often a slight sweetness that makes them particularly good with spicy food.

HELL-ISH LAGERS

Ask for 'Hell' in a German bar and you might think the barman would just turn up the Ump-pa-pa band on the sound system and invite everyone dressed in Lederhosen to come and dance with you. In fact, he'll do nothing more than pour you a pale, golden lager. The name might suggest some sort of wickedly strong brew, but in fact Hell (or Helles) is one of the palest-coloured and lowest-alcohol lagers found in Germany. Many American brewpubs make Helles-style lagers.

PILSNER

The term 'Pilsner' (or 'Pils') has been used and abused to such an extent that some people mistakenly believe it must be some sort of brand name. Born in the town of Pilsen, in what was once Bohemia (now the Czech Republic), Pilsner was the first clear, golden lager to break the dark-beer mould. This is a hoppy style of lager, both in terms of aromatics and the level of dry bitterness in the mouth. Unfortunately, most of the non-Czech versions tend to, er, take the Pils rather than make any attempt to emulate it.

BOCK

Bock beers are strong, darkish-coloured German lagers with a strong, malty flavour and (sometimes) an edge of sweetness. Originally they were made with long-distance travel in mind (the beer, not the drinker), but today the style serves more of a winter-drinking purpose. Sweeter versions are often served with desserts.

RICE-BASED LAGERS

A large number of lager-brewers use rice as one of the grain components in their ingredients list. Sometimes, in the case of many large US brands, this is more for financial purposes than for reasons of taste, but when rice is used well, it can produce a clean, crisp style of lager. Many Asian lagers – particularly Japanese – have a very distinctive flavour and body because of their use of rice.

STYLE-FREE LAGERS

This bracket covers the majority of lager made around the world. If you were served one of these blind, you would be hard-pressed to pin down where it had come from because it has no aroma or flavour, little character, and absolutely no discernible style. All you can say about this type of lager is that it is wet, cold, gassy and alcoholic.

EXTRA-COLD LAGERS

This is not so much a style by flavour as it is a style built on temperature, and no country has mastered the art of cold lager like Australia has. Refrigerated glasses, insulated bottle-holders, bottle shops as chilly as meat-packing factories... every effort and innovation has been employed to make sure you can't taste what you drink. This style of lager is used purely to quench the thirst and cool the body.

Exotic beers made in less-exotic places

Gurkha

A lager that kills the thirst other brands can't reach. Gurkha's original Nepalese flavour will creep up on you unannounced and hit you on the back of the throat with a clean slice of Challenger hop. Brewed in the foothills of the Pennines.

Sal

The taste of island life. A tropical lager made from an original Maldivian recipe using desalinated seawater and hydroponic hops. Brewed under supervision in Bradford.

Patagonia
The best a gaucho can get. A lager with a distinct Latin taste made by fourth-generation Welsh farmers in a remote corner of Argentina. Brewed under licence in Warrington.

Yakutska
The original 'ice lager'. A very-cold-fermented Siberian lager with all the clean, refreshing taste of a beer brewed in naturally cold conditions. Brewed in Scotland.

Lagers under licence

Look inside the refrigerator of your average booze shop, and the chances are high that you'll find a lagery line-up of exotic destinations. Bottles of Fosters from Australia, Kingfisher from India, maybe a brand from the Caribbean and, lurking at the back, something unpronounceable from a part of the world you thought had absolutely no brewing tradition. Yes, this fridge is your passport to foreign flavour, an international gateway to chilled refreshment.

But wait a minute. Take a closer look at the small print on some of those labels and you might find that some of those exotic destinations aren't quite so exotic after all. Under the usual blurb about 'clean, distinctive taste' and 'brewed according to an authentic recipe', I bet you'll find the depressing announcement 'brewed under licence' written in conveniently minute letters. It turns out that your Cobra lager is about as authentically Indian as chicken tikka masala.

Brewing under licence is not a new phenomenon – Danish lager

Carlsberg has been brewed in England since the 1970s – but what started as a series of minor defections has turned into a fizzy flood. As sales of lager have taken off, so the big brands have looked to reduce their costs by producing the beer in breweries closer to the main markets. You just get another company to pay for the rights to brew your beer, send them the recipe and bingo! Just like the Bionic Man, they can rebuild it.

So should we be worried about all this? Does lager – like wine – need to have a sense of place, or should we accept that big-brand lager really is no different from Pepsi and Coke and that the exact point of manufacture is of no significance? I mean, how many people actually think about flavour when they're tipping back the little green bottle?

The answer is not many, but it is worth considering what effect this brewing-under-licence phenomenon is having on other beers. The more Fosters and Buds that are granted citizenship on their travels, the greater the pressure on small-scale, locally brewed beers that can't compete with these heavily marketed products. A bar filled with nothing but faux-foreign lagers would be a very sad bar indeed.

We can rebuild it

To make any replica beer, in theory all you need is the same barley, hops, yeast and water that were used in the original. The first three on that list won't be a problem, and with a bit of tinkering, you should be able to roughly replicate the water.

The Japanese beer Kirin is brewed under licence in Europe, and the brand-owners make every effort to ensure the copies taste as close to the Oriental original as possible, even down to sending over a Japanese brewmaster to check everything is being done right. Having tasted both, I'd say you'd have to have an amazingly acute palate or far too little going on in your social life to notice any differences between the two.

Yes, of course, there are plenty of examples of licenced beers tasting inferior to their parent brews (most of the Australians, for a start), but

equally there are strong cases for arguing that a copy sometimes tastes better than the original. The British version of Yixing might be marginally different (thanks to the use of Cornish water) from its Chinese parent, but I guarantee it will be a nicer drinking experience. Lager is a pretty resilient traveller, but the quicker the time (and shorter the distance) between brewery and market, the better it will be.

Lagers brewed under licence outside their countries of origin

- Bajan (Barbados)
- Budweiser (US)
- Carlsberg (Denmark)
- Cobra (India)
- Coors (US)
- Fosters (Australia)
- Grolsch (Netherlands)
- Kingfisher (India)
- Kirin (Japan)
- Kronenbourg (France)
- Labatt's (Canada)
- Lal Toosan (India)
- Molson (Canada)
- Red Stripe (Jamaica)
- Steinlager (New Zealand)
- Stella Artois (Belgium)
- XXXX (Australia)
- Yixing (China)

The lager family line-up

The alcohol-free lager

Who on earth drinks this stuff? Reforming lager addicts? Teetotal lager louts? Airline pilots who want a drink the night before they take-off? Well, whoever they are, they can't be enjoying themselves. Alcohol has a taste and a feel all of its own, so as soon you take it out of a drink it's as obvious as taking nicotine out of a cigarette. Alcohol-free lager tastes like beer-flavoured water shoved through a carbonation machine.

The 'session' lager

Possibly the favourite target market of the giant breweries is the session drinker. This chap (for invariably it is a chap) never likes to have an empty glass in front of him, and with long-distance quaffing in mind, chooses a lager that is easy to drink (flavour and bitterness are minimal) and that can be drunk in large volumes (alcohol levels are low). The lager makes a bigger impact on your bladder than your taste buds.

The designer lager

During the 1980s – a decade not exactly renowned for its sartorial elegance – a flash new Asian lager began to appear in select bars and nightclubs in London. Its name was Sapporo, and as well as setting off a 'badge-drinking' trend, it also spawned a stream of designer lagers. To score top points, the designer lager needs to have excellent packaging, exotic origins or stylish connections (the Tate Modern has its own bottled lager now) and limited availability. Quality is an optional extra.

The weight-watcher's lager

Lite lager – one that has fewer calories in it, thanks to all the sugars being fully fermented out – is up there (or should that be down there?) with fat-free crisps in my list of products to be extremely wary of. If you want to control your waistline, my advice is to just drink less of the normal stuff.

The strong lager

The favourite tipple of the man on the street (as in the man who drinks on the street), the super-strength lager is an extremely efficient anaesthetic but not a particularly enjoyable taste experience. Often boasting alcohol levels of up to nine percent abv, it has a noticeable sweetness and viscosity which. If not served in an extremely chilly state, it can leave a rather nasty aftertaste at the back of the throat.

The big-brand lager
Made in breweries the size of oil refineries (usually nowhere near its country of origin), the big-brand lager is as ubiquitous as Coca-Cola. Pubs, parties, outdoor festivals... it crops up everywhere. No matter what label it has, the taste (or lack of) will be exactly the same. As a cold, fizzy thirst-quencher it does a pretty good job, but if it is flavour and character you are looking for, a few life-saving squirts of lime cordial will definitely be required.

The connoisseur's lager
Ideally, this will be a lager made in one of the two homes of lager-making (Germany and the Czech Republic), or, if not, it will have at least been made using traditional methods. It will be served in a tall glass, it will have a decent strength, it will be either golden or dark, and it will have some nice

malty flavour and a good, dry, hoppy aftertaste. Most importantly of all, it will stimulate the mouth and the mind as much as the bladder.

The green lager
At the same time as German researchers have been doing trials on special genetically modified yeast cultures that can give lager a longer-lasting head, a growing number of brewers are going down the green road by making organic lager. These don't taste particularly different from a non-organic lager (nor do they guarantee a cleaner hangover), but they do allow you to drink with a clearer conscience.

The gimmicky lager
In the fickle world of lager-drinking, the marketing men are always on the hunt for a new way of luring the fashion-conscious quaffer. Ice beer, chill-filtered, special dry... there have been various 'revolutionary' new techniques developed to create supposedly purer, smoother lagers. They do taste different from their traditional counterparts but only in the sense that they have less taste.

World beer: a rough guide

AUSTRALIA

Great wine, shame about the beer. Apart from one isolated island of aledom called Coopers, this country is a depressing expanse of bland, amber nectar. Coopers bottle-conditioned sparkling ale is a life-saving antidote to the lager blues.

KEY DESTINATION: The Sail and Anchor brewpub in Fremantle, Western Australia.

BELGIUM

No round-the-world beer ticket could afford to miss out this country. Wheat beers, fruit beers, Trappist beers, abbey beers, Lambic beers... if you want to taste the Bordeaux and burgundy of beer, then this is definitely where to come. They serve it like wine, treat is as seriously as wine, and sometimes they even make it taste like wine.

KEY DESTINATION: Head for the region of Payottenland for some wild Lambic flavour.

CZECH REPUBLIC

Birthplace of Pilsner and home to some of the best lagers in the world, a bar crawl around the Czech Republic will leave you vowing never to touch the XXXX again.

KEY DESTINATION: Most people don't get beyond Prague, but real lager aficionados will want to visit the Pilsner Urquell brewery in Pilsen.

ENGLAND

Although suffering the effects of a lager invasion, this is still an ale stronghold and home to a bewildering variety of cask-conditioned beers. Mild, bitter, pale ale, brown ale, stout, porter... if you can't find a style you like here, you may as well give up and return to the bland, fizzy stuff.

KEY DESTINATION: If it's brewing history you want, Burton-on-Trent is the place to go.

FRANCE

The wine culture dominates here, but there are good lagers made in Alsace-Lorraine. Up towards the Belgian border, there are many artisan microbreweries making strong, fruity *bière de garde*.

KEY DESTINATION: The region of Nord-Pas de Calais is where you will find delicious, handcrafted, warm-fermented beers.

GERMANY

Hell, Dunkel, Pils, Bock... this country has a style of lager for every mood and every food. Along with football and cars, they take beer extremely seriously in this country, so don't try asking for a lager at the bar unless you want to spend some time in the storeroom.

KEY DESTINATION: Bavaria is beer-drinking heaven, and if you can coordinate your visit with the Munich Oktoberfest, you can taste everything without moving.

IRELAND

Home to the best stout in the world and boasting a pub culture second to none. Consumption levels are such that the Guinness is as fresh as it gets.

KEY DESTINATION: Soaking up the *craic* in Dublin is top of life's 'must do' list.

JAPAN

As well as being home to some distinctive, drier styles of lager, Japan is also one of the few places in the world where you can find black beers that are brewed like a lager.

KEY DESTINATION: Visit the beer village next to Kirin's Yokohama brewery.

MEXICO

Look beyond the ubiquitous Sol and Corona styles, and you'll discover that this is one of the few places still making the dark, Vienna-style lagers. Try Dos Equis and Negra.

KEY DESTINATION: Yukatan peninsula.

SCOTLAND

There has been a major revival in ale-brewing in the last decade and a re-emergence of the old 'shilling' form of beer branding: the higher the number, the stronger the beer.

KEY DESTINATION: The Caledonian Brewery Company in Edinburgh is making some of the country's most exciting beers.

USA

Thanks to a vibrant microbrewery industry, this is now one of the most exciting beer destinations in the world. Head to the West Coast, where you'll find everything from wheat beer to porter and IPA.

KEY DESTINATIONS: Portland, Oregon, the mecca for micro-maniacs. And if you're in Austin, Texas, look out for the Celis Brewery, where Pierre Celis makes a superb range of Belgian-style beers.

Ale: one big, hoppy family

When I first started drinking beer, you were either a lager-drinker or an ale-drinker, and apart from the odd seasonal migration to the opposition camp, loyalty to the cause was rarely broken. Yes, I know, memory tends to blur reality, but back in those days of fogged-up drinking goggles and tribal imbibing, the divisions seemed very clear. Ale-drinkers played rugby and treated beer consumption as some sort of post-match rite of passage, while lager-drinkers played football and worried about whether the lime cordial was best added before or after the pint was poured. Ale-drinkers sang totally unprintable beer-drinking songs; lager-drinkers put money in the jukebox. Ale-drinkers had beer bellies, lager-drinkers had, well, gassy bellies.

Losing your cherry

Most importantly of all, though, I remember a big difference between the two camps' drinking apprenticeship. The first-ever sip of lager was not a particularly unpleasant or memorable experience, and once over that hurdle, there was basically nothing more to learn.

Losing your ale virginity, on the other hand, invariably involved a fair amount of embarrassment (like having your dad sitting by your side) and some very strange taste sensations that, gradually, you grew to understand and like. Compared with the simple lager driving test, passing your ale examination was definitely a far trickier business.

Of course, the great global beer family can't be split quite as easily as my simple parting of the drinkers. If any broad classification can be made, it is usually done according to where the yeasts work their magical thing (top- or bottom-fermenting), but since this is meant to be a jargon-free zone, I'm sticking to my old lager vs ale picture. I know some beers don't like being shoved in with the ale crowd, so in the spirit of peacekeeping, the following section will carry the alternative heading 'beers you wouldn't want to squirt lime cordial into'.

What's in a name?

The word 'ale' doesn't crop up in conversation as much as lager, and if you asked a selection of world drinkers to give a definition, you'd end up with a very strange picture of what it's meant to be. Some countries regard ale as simply a beer with a longer history; others see it as something that is stronger than the average lager. In Britain, you might get a confusing answer like 'Ale is beer, but lager isn't' (although in parts of Yorkshire they'll probably think you are talking about those frozen lumps of ice that occasionally fall from the sky).

Winning the style challenge

Ales might be based on the same basic ingredients as lagers, but that is as close as these two families get. Compared with lagers, ales tend to have more colour, aroma and flavour, they tend to be less gassy, they are usually served at a higher temperature, and they encompass a far wider range of styles: mild to bitter, pale to brown, dark ones with white, creamy heads, aromatic ones, fruity ones. If you had to choose between ale and lager to take to your desert island, I know which one I'd take – and it wouldn't be the immediately refreshing option.

Yet despite all these great attributes, ales are having a bit of a crisis of confidence at the moment. Even with the resurgence of the microbrewery movement in Britain and the US, and the encouraging success of bottle-conditioned ales, heavily marketed lagers are still winning the battle of the drip-trays. In Britain – often considered to be the home of ale – cask-conditioned ales now account for less than 10 percent of total draught beer sales.

Whether it is an image problem – ale is still seen as being as unsexy as the average darts player's physique – or a change in tastes (flavourlessness sells), one thing is certain: if the current trend continues, if breweries keep closing and ales keep disappearing, we will end up losing something a lot more significant than just a few beer-drinking songs.

Real ale vs unreal ale

Just as wine is a living, breathing thing until the moment someone yanks the cork out, so there is a type of beer that remains alive and kicking right up until the moment it is poured. This beer is known as real ale.

Over the years, some strange preconceptions have built up about real ale and real-ale-drinkers. A lot of people still think that real ale is warm, flat and cloudy and that real-ale-drinkers are bearded men with the girth of a Sumo wrestler. The reality is rather different: real ale is in fact served cool, lightly sparkling and clear, and you don't need facial hair and a beer belly to enjoy it.

Here's one I made earlier

Making real ale goes something like this. You start with a tank of fermented beer, often called 'green beer' because of its youthful state (not its colour). At this stage, you could zap this immature character into submission with a double whammy of pasteurization and filtration and send it off to the pub in a nice, safe and stable condition.

But if you believe in the concept of real ale, you'll ignore all that and put it straight into casks with a small dose of sugar. What you're aiming for here is exactly the same process that occurs in a Champagne bottle – only you want the reactivation (or second fermentation) to create a nice, gentle sparkle rather than a rampant mousse. Like Champagne, you want your beer to evolve and grow up into something far more interesting than what was originally put inside the container.

TLC required

There is one small problem with live liquids, and that is that they require delicate handling. Real ale needs to be stored properly (cool and hygienic conditions), handled carefully, and served in a way that brings out all those fresh, living aromas and flavours.

Sell it too early and it won't have finished fermenting; sell it too late and it'll be flat, tired and undrinkable. In many ways, it needs all the tender loving care you'd give to an expensive bottle of wine.

Unfortunately, the phrase 'TLC' tends to make an inconvenient smudge on an account sheet, and in today's cut-throat, shareholder-appeasing drinks business, real ale is seen to be a frustratingly efficient way to reduce profits. Big breweries want to make beer that is ready to drink as soon as it arrives at its destination, that can look after itself, that has a long shelf-life, that doesn't offend anyone and that tastes exactly the same, pint after pint. To put it simply: big breweries want to make keg beer.

Cold and creamy

Keg beer starts life at exactly the same point as a real ale, but at that 'green' stage we talked about, the beer is chilled and filtered to remove all yeast, and pasteurized to make it sterile. Essentially, the beer has been neutered to stop it behaving strangely at a later stage, and – just as you'd expect from something that's been cut off in its prime – the effects on the aroma and flavour are profound. Pasteurization tends to reduce the natural flavours of a beer and then add back its own less-appealing signature.

To get around this problem, keg beers are injected with a mixture of carbon dioxide and nitrogen to give them a visually pleasing, thick, creamy head and smooth texture, and they are served nice and cold so no one will notice that they don't actually taste of very much. Keg beers (sometimes called 'nitro-keg', 'smoothflow' or 'creamflow' beers) are less challenging, more profitable, easier to drink, and harder to get passionate about.

In an ideal world, real ale and keg beer would happily co-exist like *terroir* wines and branded wines. But as the beer industry becomes more and more fixated by heavily marketed pints of creamy, big-headed beers, the continued existence of real ales becomes more and more precarious. This is why, in the UK, we have an organization called the Campaign for Real Ale (or CAMRA), whose membership is at an all-time high. Hopefully, they will still have something to campaign about in years to come.

Bitter or mild, sir?

BITTER

Among the many things that Americans find quaint but rather strange about the British is our curious habit of going up to the bar and asking for a pint of bitter. This one keeps them constantly amused. You can see them standing there, scratching their heads, trying to work out who came up with this bizarre system of drinks classification and whether – if they wait long enough – someone will eventually come up and ask for a pint of sour or a pint of sweet.

The name 'bitter' has soaked into the British beer-drinker's vocabulary to the extent that a lot of people mistakenly believe it is a completely separate drink from ale. As its name suggests, bitter is indeed slightly bitter. The nickname was given to a style of beer that emerged at the turn of the last century, a style that was characterized by its dry, tangy flavour of hops. Compared with its traditional pale-ale cousin, bitter was generally darker in colour and lower in alcohol, and it left a far more distinct aftertaste in your mouth.

Learning to drink it has always been some sort of male rite of passage – somewhere between losing your virginity and owning your first car, you will have to get through your first pint of bitter. And although the first gulp will invariably cause a facial expression normally reserved for eating porridge, you will soon grow to admire this strange but loveable brew.

Today, it is still the main style of ale sold across Britain, and apart from a common 'hoppy' thread, the term 'bitter' covers a multitude of different colours, aromas, flavours and strengths. Many breweries make two or three different versions at different levels of alcohol, often with a confusing (confusing if you aren't a local, that is) system of prefixes like 'Ordinary', 'Best', 'Special', 'Extra Special'. The more you drink, the easier it is to understand.

And despite (or perhaps because of) their amusement at this quintessentially British drink, many American microbreweries are now making bitter, too.

MILD

Mention the word 'mild' and it conjures up images of men in flat caps rolling cigarettes with thick, calloused fingers, of pint mugs with handles, and of ploughman's lunches that were actually big enough to satisfy a ploughman's appetite.

Unfortunately, like all three things just mentioned, mild has become as hard to find as a pub that serves pork scratchings. There is a real danger that, as the lager flood continues to rise, this old style of ale will eventually disappear for good.

Mild dates back to the 19th century, when almost all beer was brown in colour and brewers began developing a new version that used fewer hops and was therefore 'milder' in taste. Although they also tended to be lower in alcohol, the term 'mild' related to the brew's lack of bitterness rather than to any lack of strength.

Mild was a drink for the workers. Not only was it cheaper than other beers, but it was also an ale designed to quench the thirst and – in theory – be weak enough so that you could sup a few pints of mild at lunchtime and still be able to work in the afternoon without falling asleep on the job. In addition, these were beers with a lot of flavour, so that even if your tastebuds had been numbed into submission by dirty factory air, you would still be able to taste the strong, malty character of mild.

This style of beer can still be found in areas once dominated by heavy industry, but in an age when moving a mouse is the commonest form of work exercise, mild is seen as being an old-fashioned beer with a shrinking (and ageing) market.

With many American micros taking up the challenge, however, a mild revival might not be just a pipe dream. At a time when health concerns and drink-driving laws are making people look to lower-alcohol options – and when real-ale brewers desperately need an easy-drinking ale to lure in bitter-resistant drinkers – mild looks like the perfect pint for the job.

Pale ale vs brown ale

BROWN ALE

Back in 1927, an advertisement for a new beer appeared in the *Newcastle Journal*. 'It's just the right strength,' went the first line, 'not too heavy for summer drinking, yet with sufficient body to satisfy the man who likes a good ale and knows when he gets it.' Copywriters could get away with things like that back then.

The beer, if you hadn't already guessed, was Newcastle Brown Ale, and even its creator – a man called Colonel James Porter – couldn't have predicted how successful it was to become. Today, more than 35 million bottles are exported every year (the Chinese refer to it as the 'gentleman's beer') and although domestic sales have slipped a bit, the 'broon bottle' can still be found in almost every student-union bar in the land.

Launched at a time when most other beers were dark, full-bodied brews, this reddish, malty ale immediately became a hit with local shipbuilders and munitions workers, who wanted a beer to quench their post-work thirst. Most of the industry might have since disappeared, but the Geordies' love of Porter's nutty ale has never weakened. With its distinctive packaging and various daft nicknames, the beer has become inextricably linked with the Tyne, and in particular with Newcastle United's Toon Army.

In Britain, there are many other good examples of this style of beer – Samuel Smith, for instance, makes an excellent version called Nut Brown Ale. Although there is a sweeter, 'southern' style of brown ale, it is the drier, more refreshing northern version that has inspired brewers around the world.

Rumour has it that some American brewers have even sent representatives to a Sunderland brewing school to try and work out how to emulate the original. Good versions are made (without such assistance, I might add) by the New York-based Brooklyn Brewery, Pete's Brewing Company in California and Rogue in Oregon.

PALE ALE

If you had to choose the most confused (and confusing) member of the beer family, it would have to be pale ale.

To some people, it's just a bottled version of a bitter; to others, it's a strong beer with a distinctive, high level of hop character. Then there are a few brewers who seem to think a pale ale can join the club simply by being of pale-ish complexion. The truth is that most pale ales are bottled, most are amber-red in colour, and most taste like a hoppier version of a bitter.

The history of pale ale is closely linked to the town of Burton-on-Trent, where a combination of a particular type of water (high in salts) and an innovative new system of brewing (one that cleared the beer of yeast) helped create a new style of clear beer. Before lagers came along and stole the show, pale ale was not only the most refreshing beer on the block, it was also one of the most widely travelled, refreshing parts of the world

that other beers could only dream of reaching.

The most famous pale ale (and one of the greatest British exports of all time) was India Pale Ale (IPA for short). During the height of the British Empire, brewers were asked to come up with a beer that would be robust enough to survive months at sea but still remain thirst-quenching enough to keep overheated expats happy. The answer was a strong, heavily hopped beer whose alcohol and hops acted as preservatives on the long sea journey.

IPA eventually became a style in its own right. In recent years, it has enjoyed a strong revival – albeit in a rather toned-down form, since today's drinkers do not have the same taste for the heavily hopped beers of old. In the US, there is an equally strong pale-ale movement, and should you travel to Washington State, you're likely to discover that it's easier to find an IPA there than in many parts of Britain (so who said colonials didn't have their uses?).

Stouts and porters

It took a long time before I had the courage to order my first pint of Guinness. As a teenager, I'd look at these white-topped, black-bodied glasses and wonder a) what on earth must they taste like, and b) how come it took so long to pour the damn things?

Eventually, curiosity – and the fact that the black-pint brigade invariably seemed to be having a better time than the pale-pint mob – pushed me into giving it a go. From the first cold, creamy mouthful I was hooked. Here was a beer that not only looked better than any other beer behind the bar, but it was served with more style, tasted and felt like nothing else and somehow managed to pull off a final trick of being just as thirst-quenching as a lager. The day you discover stout is the day you can finally take off your beer-drinking stabilizers and say you've arrived.

There is a lot of confusion over the difference between porter and stout, but before splitting them apart, let's look at what joins them together. They are both dark beers made from highly roasted malts, and so both tend to have flavours at the chocolate and coffee end of the spectrum. Both styles have long histories, both have managed to reach countries a long way from their birthplaces and both are currently enjoying a remarkable return to fashion.

PORTER

Until its revival at the end of the 1970s, porter had almost completely disappeared in the UK. It began its life in London at the start of the 18th century. Its name is thought to relate either to its popularity with market porters, or to the fact that this style emerged at a time when beer started to be delivered (by porters) from breweries to pubs. Originally, it would have been a cloudy, dark-brown beer; the blacker versions we know today didn't start life until a century later, when roasting techniques had improved.

Porter reached its peak during the industrial revolution; as the British Empire spread, so the beer followed. Until recently, it was often the case that porter was better understood (and respected) in obscure places like Estonia and China than it was in the country

that created it. But thanks to
a few determined breweries and
campaigning organizations such as
CAMRA, the once national favourite
has made a strong comeback.

STOUT

Meanwhile, stout has been riding
the Irish pub wave and is now more
fashionable that it ever was. The
roots of this beer are linked to what
would once have been a family of
porters. In the days when brewers
used to make a variety of styles of
porter, the most full-bodied ones
(the 'stoutest' versions) became
known as stout.

Guinness started life as something
called Extra Stout Porter, and
thanks to a combination of clever
marketing, licenced brewing, and its
strong national identity (Irishness
sells), it has become one of the most
widely recognized beer brands in the
world. While keeping the purists
happy with its draught and bottle-
conditioned versions, Guinness has
never been afraid to branch out and
create new stout-drinking markets,
whether by way of floating widgets
in cans or bottles or tweaking the
temperature at which it is served.

Dry stouts such as Guinness
(and its Irish competitors Beamish
and Murphys) are instantly
recognizable by their black, opaque
appearance, their inch-thick head
of creamy bubbles, their strong,
coffee-chocolate flavours and their
distinctive, dry, bitter bite. These are
refreshing beers, but they are also
tangy, and it is this tangy quality that
makes them good partners for food.

One of the most renowned stout
matches is with oysters. In fact, the
two go so well together that some
brewers have been known to add
some of the liquid found in oyster
shells (or in some cases, whole
oysters) into the brew to create a
style of beer known as 'oyster stout'.
From the few I've tasted, I'd say that,
apart from a slight briny quality to
the taste, it's hard to tell that a fishy
ingredient has been used.

Three other styles of stout exist:
sweet 'milk' stout is made with milk
sugars; oatmeal stouts use small
additions of oatmeal to make a
silkier, smoother beer; and imperial
stouts are big, strong, tarry beers
still being made in parts of Eastern
Europe and Scandinavia.

Fruit beers

Apart from our good friends in Belgium (where real men drink cherry beer with their quiche), most unreconstructed males still reckon fruit beers have a bit of an image problem. They'll happily shove a wedge of lime into the neck of their lager bottle and they'll feel no embarrassment when someone drops a slice of lemon into their Hoegaarden, but suggest they try a bright-red glass of *frambozen*, and it's as if you've asked them to take up Morris dancing.

If you are in this group – and I'm optimistically assuming you are still reading this page – you are missing out on some of the most refreshing and fascinating beers in the world. In fact, fruit beers are beers that take time, effort and a lot of skill to make, that smell as wonderful as they taste, that quench the thirst and get the gastric juices flowing.

They may sound like some sort of wine/beer hybrid (and often they taste like it), but they are actually nothing more than a conventional beer with fruit added as another fermentable ingredient and flavouring. The most famous are those found in the Belgian Lambic family of brews, where the use of wild yeast adds a lovely winey character to the characteristic sweet-and-sour flavours.

How to have your cherries and drink them

Kriek (or cherry beer) is the best-known Belgian fruit beer, and, traditionally, it is made with the hard Schaarbeek cherry. The fruit is picked late so that the flavours are concentrated, and there is plenty of sugar to set off a second fermentation when the cherries are poured into the barrels of beer.

The skins of the cherries add tannin to the beer, while the stones help give a pleasant almond edge to its flavour. To make a *frambozen*, you just follow the same process, but use ripe raspberries rather than cherries.

With their strong, fruity flavours and refreshing tartness, these beers make perfect summer drinks and aperitifs. The sweeter versions can also be drunk with desserts.

What does Lambic mean?

Lambic is one of the oldest styles of beer in the world. Instead of using the cultured yeast favoured by most commercial beer producers, Lambic brewers leave their beer (and livelihoods) in the lap of the wild-yeast gods. Fermentation is spontaneous, production methods are traditional, and flavours are rustic. Most Lambic beers come from Belgium, but there are a few brave, adventurous souls who are going native in other countries.

How to make Lambic-style fruit beer (as told by an Englishman)

They say the English are renowned for their eccentricity, and there is surely nothing more eccentric than a bunch of Englishmen making Lambic-style apricot and strawberry beers in a medieval brewery in deepest Lincolnshire.

According to Steve Barrett, head brewer at Melbourn Brothers, the beers can be made only between October and May, because during the warmer months, you can't control the fermentation and there are too many spores and moulds around to let the wild yeasts do their job. You need quite a sour, astringent beer as your base to counteract the sweetness of the fruit; you need at least three months for the beer to ferment; then you need at least six months for it to mature. It's time-consuming, it's mucky (wild yeasts don't like clean breweries), it's risky (acetic-acid bacteria love fruit beers) and it's expensive. But it's also utterly delicious.

Famous fruit beers from around the world

MELBOURN BROS APRICOT (UK) A beautifully aromatic beer from the wild side of Lincolnshire.

LIEFMAN'S KRIEK (BELGIUM) Sweet-and-sour heaven in the famous tissue-wrapped bottle.

CANTILLON DRY ROSÉ DE GRAMBRINUS (BELGIUM) A classic blend of *kriek* and *frambozen*.

ST PETER'S BREWERY ELDERBERRY BEER (UK) Floral-scented refreshment from another great British microbrewery.

SAMUEL ADAMS CRANBERRY (US) A tart, refreshing summer beer from Boston.

ROGUE 'N' BERRY (US) The Oregon-based Rogue microbrewery makes a fruity beer with local marion berries.

Wheat beers

At around the same time that wine-drinkers decide it is warm enough to open the first rosé of the year, beer-drinkers usually head towards their own distinctively coloured form of refreshment. The name of this warm-weather target is wheat beer, and, unlike rosé, it is fast becoming one of the most fashionable drinks on the international bar menu.

As the name suggests, wheat beers (or 'white beers', as they are often known) are made using a significant proportion of wheat in the grain mix. The result is a pale, peach-coloured beer with fruity aromas and a distinctive, almost bubblegum-ish flavour. They are usually bottle-fermented, which – along with their lively effervescence – has helped them win the tag 'Champagne of the beer world'.

This is a beer with a long history. Over four centuries ago, German wheat beer was being brewed exclusively by the Bavarian royal family (common folk were not allowed wheat for brewing), but it wasn't until the 1800s that a man by the name of Georg Schneider obtained a licence to brew it commercially.

People grew fond of these citric, slightly tart beers, but they weren't exactly bestsellers. A combination of lager competition, the hassle factor (wheat beers are messier and harder to make than barley-based beers) and their association with pensioners and denture-less supping meant that wheat beers struggled to find a mainstream market.

But then, in the 1980s, they suddenly gained cult status with Germany's younger drinkers. Thanks to this new image and the success of the Belgian white beer Hoegaarden, wheat beer suddenly became the thinking-man's lager. Today, new versions of the cloudy one are being brewed all around the world, and as is the way when something becomes fashionable, there are as many pale imitations as authentically hazy copies.

Is it a lager or an ale?
Because it tends to be served at a lager temperature and because it looks like a (cloudy) lager and tastes

as refreshing as a lager, many drinkers mistakenly believe wheat beer must be made like lager. In fact, these pale beers are fermented like ales, but – owing to their un-ale-like ingredients – tend to occupy their own separate category in the beer world. So there you go: brewed like ale, chilled like lager, tastes like nothing else.

Clear or cloudy?

Some people are put off drinking wheat beers because of their hazy appearance, and a few brewers produce clear, filtered versions (labelled *Kristall Weizen*) to keep the cloudy-phobics happy. But in the case of wheat beer, cloudy means good, not bad; to get the full, fruity, yeast-boosted flavour of this style of beer, you need to drink the bottle-fermented versions that contain sediment in the bottle. Just as unfiltered wines have become popular with drinkers who don't like flavour-stripped products, so sediment-rich wheat beers are by far the most popular style.

The Hoegaarden effect

Up until the 1960s, wheat beers were bumbling along in their own cult niche with their own small devoted band of 'wheaties'. Outside Belgium and Germany, it was just as hard to find a wheat beer as it was to find someone who understood what they were. But then, sometime during the decade of flower power and flares, a Belgian called Pierre Celis decided to make his own donation to the school of peace, love and understanding by rejuvenating a style of beer that had once dominated the brewing landscape of his homeland. The spice-flavoured white beer he created was called Hoegaarden, and its subsequent success helped wheat beer find international commercial stardom.

A slice of lemon with that?

Just as not all bottles of Mexican lager require a wedge of lime stuffed down their necks, there is no rule that says wheat beer must come with a slice of lemon – although try telling that to bartenders. Personally, I think fruit garnishes are for cocktails; wheat beers have a nice enough bite to them already without further citric assistance.

Cult beers

Step outside the mainstream flow of lagers and ales, and you'll find a range of esoteric beers whose production methods are distinctly different, whose flavours are off-centre and whose distribution is often extremely limited. In volume terms, these beers are insignificant blips on the world beer radar, but in quality terms, they stand out like giants wading through a deluge of bland commercial products.

Australian sparkling ale
In a sea of blander nectar, a small clutch of Adelaide-based breweries stick their necks out for the cause of ale. The most famous is Coopers, and although production is not exactly cult-like, the devoted following it has built up around the world certainly warrants its inclusion in the cult club. These bottle-conditioned beers are cloudy and have a characteristic fruitiness not dissimilar to some wheat beers.

Barley wine
This is an old style of English ale whose only connection with wine comes from its high alcohol strength and often winey flavour. Dark-coloured, rich and malty, barley wines are the late-night sippers of the beer world.

Foreign extra stout
Of the numerous versions of Guinness made in Ireland and around the world, foreign extra stout, or FES, is the most distinct and hard to find (if you live outside the tropics). Made by blending fresh stout and oak-aged stout, it is a strong, wild-smelling beer with a love-it-or-hate-it flavour. Extremely popular in West Africa, you can often find it in Nigerian-run restaurants in Britain.

Japanese black beer
Although more renowned for pale, dry lagers, most of the Japanese brewers also make a very dark style of lager that is thought to have originated in Germany. Occasionally the colour is so deep that the beer seems opaque, but more often it is closer to tawny, and in terms of flavour it's a bit like tasting a cross between a lager and a stout.

Lambic beers
Lambic is a very old style of beer that relies on wild, airborne yeasts

to set off fermentation. Most Lambics are made in an area called Payottenland in Belgium, but you can also find versions in France, the Netherlands and the UK. Lambic beers have a characteristic sourness even in the sweeter fruit versions.

Micro beers

Some of the most exciting beers today are those made by small-production microbreweries, whose brewing techniques are very 'hands-on'. Renowned on the West Coast of the US (particularly in Portland, Oregon), the micro movement has now spread to the UK, and the beers vary from revived old styles to brand-new, off-the-wall experiments.

Old ales

The term 'old ale' comes with no simple definition, but generally, these are strong, traditional-style beers that have either been aged before release or are bottled with the aim of being laid down like a wine. Old ales make great gifts for collectors who don't have a wine-exclusivity clause on their cellar doors.

Sweet stout

For those who find the bitter flavours of traditional stout too hard to swallow, there is a small band of sweetened versions that have built up a reputation for their alleged medicinal properties. The most famous of these are milk stouts – stout sweetened with lactose – and as well as being a big hit in old people's homes, they make great dessert beers.

Trappist beers

Maybe they do it to fill the day, or perhaps it's just a way of letting their hair down. Whatever the reason, monks and alcohol-creation have a long and colourful history of co-existence. Today, there are six abbeys of the Trappist order (five in Belgium and one in the Netherlands) that are still brewing beer, and their products and the term 'Trappist beer' are protected by an appellation law.

Although the styles vary and most monasteries make more than one label, the common link among these beers is that they all tend to be strong, fruity and bottle-conditioned.

Widget beers

All around the world, man is constantly pushing out the boundaries of engineering and technology. From space shuttles that can land like they've just returned from a package holiday to miniature robot submersibles that can check the cutlery in the *Titanic*'s dining room, the achievements never cease to impress.

Yet there is one invention that really makes you proud to be part of this *Homo sapiens* species, one that took years to develop and that has had a profound effect on the lives of millions. It is a device so innovative and successful that it received the Queen's Award for Technological Achievement, and it has proved so profitable that it has spawned endless copies. Ladies and gentlemen (drumroll, please), I give you the widget.

Brewing boffins

The story of the widget begins deep in the research and development department of Guinness – that purveyor of fine black beer and the art of being patient. Sometime back in the 1980s, the company's team

in white lab-coats were staring at their blackboard, wondering how they were going to solve the following riddle: what is small enough to fit inside a can and clever enough to make a take-home beer taste like a draught beer?

To understand their dilemma, you first need to understand what happens when a pint of the black stuff is poured in a pub. Draught Guinness gets its distinctive creamy head by what is known as a 'surging' effect. As the beer passes through the tap, bubbles of nitrogen and carbon dioxide break out to form that characteristic inch-thick white top. The carbon dioxide – with its larger bubbles – helps create the depth of head, while the minute nitrogen bubbles tighten it all up into a nice, lip-coating foam. Still with me? Okay, now try and work out how you transfer all that into a can.

Surging beer

After months of trials with more failed attempts (and mess) than the bouncing-bomb experiments of the Second World War, they eventually came up something called ICS, or 'in-can system', to give it its full, highly imaginative name. ICS was basically just a small, hollow plastic chamber that sat at the bottom of a 500ml can. Guinness put the gas-injected beer into the can under pressure and when you, the drinker, opened it at home, the difference in pressures forced the beer out of said chamber and through a tiny hole in its surface. *Voilà!* Le surge was created, and Guinness Draught in Cans was a reality.

Floating widgets

But this wasn't enough for the boffins. Concerned that their invention caused a surge of gas in only a small proportion of the beer, they went back to their can-strewn laboratory and eventually came up with a little device known as the floating widget. As the Guinness press release wonderfully describes it, 'The end result was a new era of widgetry.' The new free-floating system allowed more gas to be knocked through the beer, which in turn meant a bigger surge and a creamier glass of Guinness in front of your telly. Widgets like

these are now common in other types of beer that want to re-create the smooth taste of a nitro-keg beer in a can.

Bottles and roquets

The story doesn't end quite there. Over the last few years, Guinness has taken things one step further by inventing the 'rocket widget', which is used in bottles. Noticing the increasing trend towards drinking out of bottles rather than glasses, the company created a widget system that releases gas into the beer the moment the cap is taken off. Even better, the movement of the bottle reactivates the widget every time you take another swig, so that now you don't even need to pour your beer into a glass to get the taste and effect of a good head.

Of course, not everyone is exactly happy about these new developments. Thanks to the fact that you can drink a pub-style beer wherever you want now, there are a lot of pub landlords scratching their heads and moaning, 'Where *is* everyone?'

Cider-house rules

Old Knobbly Fusset

Worzel Scruncher

Rosy-cheeked Larkin

Belchington Bitter

Speckled Bruiser

William Tell Red

Chiselhurst Chunder

Knotty Grosset

Foolscap Hardy

Dingleberry Dew

Scrumpy Love

Dog Yelp

Cider: not just for those who say 'oo-arrr'

When was the last time you drank cider? Unless you live in one of the southwestern counties of England or come from Newcastle (sales of cider are huge in Geordie-land), the chances are high that it was a long time ago. You probably tried some as a teenager – I lost my drinking virginity to full-bodied scrumpy at The Royal Agricultural Show – and maybe had a brief and not particularly pleasant flirtation with it during the student Snake Bite years. But then you discovered beer and spirits, and cider was relegated to that list of drinks you vowed never to return to: an unfashionable, unwanted reminder of your early alcohol experimentation.

So where did it all go wrong for the great appley one? Go back a few hundred years and you'll find that this drink was held in higher regard than French wine. During the 17th century, English gentlemen were more likely to be seen sipping flutes of cider than glasses of claret. Back then, Redstreak cider – made from the Redstreak apple – was held in the same esteem as are the wines of Châteaux Pétrus and Lafite today.

You can still find examples of the sort of handcrafted, real farmhouse ciders that diarists such as John Evelyn used to write about in such glowing terms, but the definition and image of cider have changed completely. As defined by the UK's National Association of Cider Makers, cider is 'a beverage obtained by partial or complete fermentation of the juice of apples, or concentrated apple juice, or a mixture of such fresh and concentrated juices'. Wait, that's not all. It can also be made 'with or without the addition before or after fermentation of sugars and/or potable water', and 'provided that not more than 25 percent of the total single-strength juice content is pear', you can still call your product cider.

With a definition as ambiguous as this, is it any wonder the perception of cider is so poor? Most of the cider drunk in Britain is made in vast quantities, using imported apple concentrate, water, artificial sweeteners and preservatives. If you want to taste real cider, you have to look for the little guys who are still making it the old-fashioned way, with home-grown apple juice and as few additives as possible.

Real cider

The Campaign for Real Ale (CAMRA) has set up an organization called APPLE (answers on a postcard for what it stands for), which defines cider as 'freshly pressed apple juice naturally fermented with wild yeast, unpasteurized, unfiltered and uncarbonated'. Sounds simple, but fewer and fewer are doing it.

Single-variety ciders

Following in the footsteps of Chardonnay and Cabernet Sauvignon, a number of cider producers are now making ciders from individual varieties of apple rather than from blends of lots of different types. Anyone for a glass of Knotted Kernel?

Scrumpy

Scrumpy is basically unrefined cider that has not been filtered, hence the usual cloudy appearance. The term does not relate to alcoholic strength and, owing to the widespread use of the title for very unscrumpy-like

products, it increasingly gives little indication of style or quality.

French cider

The French have just as long a cider-making history as the English. Thanks to strict regulations, their industry has managed to maintain a single definition of what cider should be. Because they do not permit any artificial sweeteners, off-dry and sweet cider are made using an old method called keeving. This involves removing the cider from its lees, or yeast deposits, so that it doesn't ferment to full dryness. Normandy ciders are absolutely delicious.

World ciders

Although the traditional heartland of cider-making is in western Europe (Normandy, Brittany, the Basque region and England's southwestern counties), you can find versions all over the world. The UK is the biggest producer, followed by South Africa and France.

Perry

A drink made from fermented pear juice. The best ones use proper Perry pears, rather than ordinary dessert varieties.

The birth of saké

Saké: drink of the gods

Poor old saké. One of the most misunderstood beverages in the world, it just can't seem to escape its tag of 'that weird, warm stuff they serve with sushi'. Not only is there still widespread confusion as to whether it's a beer, a wine or a spirit (British Customs and Excise list it under fortified wine – which it isn't), but most of the saké served outside Japan is poor-quality, badly stored material served at completely the wrong temperature. At a time when we are eating more Asian-inspired food than ever before, it seems strange that we are neglecting a drink that matches it perfectly.

Until I sat down to write this book, my own knowledge of saké was based on nothing more than hazy memories of something hot and difficult to describe. Invariably, that memory would overestimate the alcohol level (most saké is about the strength of an Australian Shiraz) and underestimate the drink's potential to be, well, vaguely memorable.

But then I was shown the light. Not by some ancient saké-master or wrinkly old guru with a degree in rice polishing, but by a Yorkshireman called Ian Hafferty, who once sold Thomas Hardy Ale to the Japanese and now sells strange Japanese beverages (ever heard of Pocari Sweat?) to the Brits. The first thing he poured me was a cloudy saké called Nigorizake (sort of the Hoegaarden of the saké world), and one sip of this strange but deliciously creamy drink had me signing up as a fully fledged supporter of his saké sect.

Once you put the linguistic gobbledegook to one side, saké is really a very simple drink to understand. 'Made like a beer, served like a wine' is the common description, and while this is a massive generalization (Tetleys was never brewed like this), it serves as a good starting point. The four main ingredients are rice, water, yeast and something called koji, which is basically mouldy rice that helps convert the starch in rice into fermentable sugars.

Using special saké rice – you can't just bung in the basmati – the saké-master (a rice version of a winemaker) will polish the grains to remove the unwanted fats and proteins, and the more the rice is polished, the better the saké gets. The polished rice is then soaked, put into a fermenting vat with some *koji*, yeast and water and left to bubble away until you're left with a raw saké at about 20 percent abv. This alcoholic liquid is then filtered, diluted to about 15 percent abv, pasteurized and bottled.

What does saké taste like?

Good question. I'm still trying to work that one out. It's easy to bandy around words such as 'delicate', 'light', 'soft' and 'off-dry', but when it comes to pinning down exact aromas and flavours, it all gets a bit tricky. Some sakés have a prominent aroma, while others seem completely neutral. Some have flavours at the earthy-nutty end of the spectrum, others – like the sediment-rich Nigorizake style – have an extra-creamy dimension to them. They say saké has 400 flavour components compared with wine's 200, but I'm still struggling to identify 10.

Saké knowledge

- Saké is thought to have originated in China, not Japan.
- Saké is brewed across Asia.
- Rumour has it that it all started when someone spat out their rice and someone cleaning it up later, found the lump had started to ferment.
- Premium saké should be served chilled.
- Saké is best drunk as young and fresh as possible.
- Saké reputedly causes few hangovers (yeah, right!).
- In America, they now have micro-sakéries (like microbreweries) where small batches of fresh, unpasteurized saké are made.
- An American company called SakéOne has developed a line of flavoured sakés.
- Soaking in a bath of saké is good for the circulation (but then, so is hot water, and it's a darn sight cheaper...).
- Saké can be used to make some wickedly good cocktails. My favourite is the Saké Margarita, using saké instead of Tequila. Just mix dry saké with Triple Sec and lime juice, shake with ice and serve.

BOOZY
SITUATIONS

Party booze

Hosting a party can be stressful enough that you almost need to hold one to celebrate getting through one. Will enough people turn up? Will your different circles of friends get on? Will your mad neighbours take revenge when you keep them awake all night? Will your carpet survive? Will your home smell like an ashtray for the next six months? Compared with all these concerns, any worries about booze supply will seem almost trivial. Most parties follow a familiar and rather unimaginative alcoholic route. Having made a token gesture of filling the fridge with lager, the host leaves the rest of the supply in the totally incapable hands of the guests, who invariably pitch up with whatever they could find in the late-night grocery store nearest your house. Here, then, are a few ideas to make sure the night is more like a fiesta than a siesta.

DIY flavoured vodka

Making you own flavoured vodka is easy and cheap. The most popular additions are citrus fruits (use the rind, not the flesh), vanilla (use fresh pods, not essence), chocolate (simmer the two together in a pan and skim off the fat before bottling), coffee (use whole, roasted beans) and chilli. Make sure you make them at least a few days before the party so the flavour soaks in, and remember to shake the bottles regularly.

Shooters and slammers

There is no better way of breaking the ice of a slow-starting party than with a few chilled shots of Schnapps or vodka, or a glass of Tequila helped down with a little lime and salt. The trick is to make sure you use a decent-quality spirit, and the colder it is, the better. Flaming drinks and mixed shots (like B-52s and Slippery Nipples) are an optional extra for parties with a retro theme.

Vodka ice shoots

If it's a big party and you have a reasonable budget, you can always order one of those ice sculptures where you pour the vodka in at the top and have someone waiting with their mouth open at the hole in the bottom.

Fruit punches

Easy to prepare and frighteningly easy to drink, a fruit punch is the perfect atmosphere-stoking material. To make a classic punch, you will need a good golden rum, some lime or lemon juice, sugar, fresh orange juice, various fruits to marinate in the punch itself, and some soda water. A few hours before the party, mix everything together except the soda in a big bowl. Then at the last minute add the soda water and some ice.

Alcoholic fruit

Take a watermelon and poke a hole in the top. Using a funnel or a big, needle-less syringe, fill the middle with vodka or rum. If you haven't got the patience, just cut the watermelon into slices and put them in a big bowl, pour in the vodka and let the fruit get a good soaking.

Homebrew

If you are on a tight budget, it's worth considering a little domestic brewing. Homebrew beer kits have improved dramatically (not that quality is ever an issue after the first few drinks at a party). In terms of value for money, you won't find a better volume/price ratio anywhere.

Big bottles

For the sort of party where Champagne is more appropriate than a Kamikaze, a jeroboam or methuselah will definitely make an impression, as they say in Ferrero Rocher circles. If you can't fit these massive bottles in the fridge, then simply fill the bath with cold water and ice and put them in.

Small bottles

The chic party accessory, which first appeared in London's Fashion Week a couple of years ago, is the baby bottle of Champagne, served with a straw. Ideal for the lager-drinking generation who feel undressed without a bottle in their hands and a good idea for hosts who can't afford to have spillages.

New-age soft drinks

Arriving with soft drinks (well, someone's got to drive) isn't such an embarrassment anymore – particularly if you turn up with one of the so-called new-age drinks (SoBe, Tazo, Arizona) that have taken off in the US. And if nobody drinks them, they make great rehydration material for the morning after.

Wedding booze

If you are one of the parents of the bride, the wedding reception is nothing less than *Nightmare on Catering Street*: a shocking tale of booze management involving a large, thirsty cast of different ages and social groups who have come together for the sole purpose of getting lagered at your expense. The true extent of the calamity you are facing only becomes apparent after all the other trivial but expensive challenges (dress, marquee, food) have been ticked off the list.

Suddenly, you find yourself with a budget of £1,000 to keep 100 people well lubricated for at least six hours, and you know there are at least 10 wine snobs, 15 sweet-toothed grannies, a couple of vegans and two Orthodox Jews who won't touch anything that isn't kosher. The chances of you hitting the bottle before buying a bottle are extremely high.

But don't panic just yet. I always remember the calming words someone gave me just before I stood up to nervously deliver a best man's speech: 'Remember, everyone is here to have a good time – they want to like you and laugh at your jokes.' The same applies to the booze you supply: everyone will be so busy getting high on the feel-good factor that all gastronomic quality-control buttons will pretty much be switched off for the day. I'll bet you could pour some cheap Bulgarian Cabernet into a bunch of decanters and no one would a) notice something was wrong, or b) complain if they did.

And finally, a tip for all you budding brides and grooms out there. Instead of setting up the usual boring clichéd wedding list for yourselves – you know the sort: one toaster, four pillows, a cutlery set and a matching pair of cuddly toys – why not find a wine merchant who will set up a far more interesting liquid list? You get a wine collection that would normally take years to accumulate, and your friends can buy something that seems just a little bit more meaningful than a set of carving knives.

THE DOS AND DON'TS OF WEDDING BOOZE

 DO buy in advance. Most weddings are announced months ahead of the date, so if it's a summer wedding, buy your booze in the January sales.

 DON'T feel ashamed at hiring a transit van and heading off to the nearest bulk-booze warehouse, but DO be careful not to buy bootleg material. Policemen storming into the marquee tend to be a bit of an atmosphere-dampener.

 DO buy the best sparkling wine you can rather than the cheapest Champagne you can afford. Most big-brand, premium sparkling wines – particularly those made by Champagne houses in the New World – are far better quality than those at the bottom rung of the Champagne ladder.

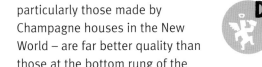 **DON'T** serve your wine in Paris goblets.

 DO serve your fizz from big bottles. Sure, size doesn't matter, but pulling out a methuselah doesn't half impress the in-laws – and it saves having to open eight smaller bottles.

 DON'T serve different (ie, better) wines on the top table. It will only spark off even more bitterness among those relations and friends who didn't make the cut.

 DO behave like a restaurateur and serve wines that your guests won't recognize. If you put well-known brands on the table, they'll all be able to work out exactly how much you've spent on them.

 DON'T provide spirits unless you're prepared for the marquee to be dismantled before the wedding has finished.

 DO go for New World rather than Old World wines. Not only will they be more reliable, but their sweeter fruit flavours will go down better with the oldies (saving you the hassle of offering an off-dry option as well).

 DON'T forget to lock your own cellar door, or the door to wherever you're keeping your own private supply. Believe me, when your guests are drunk, they still somehow always manage to find it.

Comfort booze

Is there such a thing as the perfect funeral drink? Sorry to turn such a morbid corner, but in trying to select comforting drinks, there are worse places to aim the research at than the social event which desperately needs a little liquid TLC. Some of you might say that any form of alcohol – preferably the neatest and strongest – is suitable for this black-suit, black-mood get-together. After all, it's not just feelings of sorrow you have to contend with, there are all those grim relatives you hadn't expected to bump into again until next Christmas.

FEEL-GOOD DRINKS FOR FEEL-BAD MOMENTS

While alcohol is a necessary anaesthetic at times like this, what matters most is how that alcohol is wrapped up. After all, Champagne, lager, Flaming Lamborghinis, young claret, English wine, and homebrew all deliver an alcoholic kick, but you definitely wouldn't want to serve any of these at a funeral.

So here are my suggestions for booze to get your spirits back up – and no, you don't have to wait for someone to die in order to drink them. If you've just been dumped by your partner, got fired by your boss, lost your season ticket, or just got a plain old dose of the blues, all these are guaranteed to soothe the parts other beverages fail to reach.

Big, cuddly, woolly-jumper wines

Ripe, softly textured, full-bodied reds are just what you need when it's dank and wet outside and the central heating has broken down. A bottle of Barossa Shiraz would be my first-choice potion from the vinotherapy first-aid kit, closely followed by a quick injection of Chilean Merlot, a couple of spoonfuls of California Zinfandel and maybe something from the southern Rhône to finish.

West Coast sunshine

Sometimes, all it takes to cheer you up is a simple dose of your reliable friend, Chardonnay, but it can't be any old bog-standard stuff. To get the required effect, you have to go for one of those super-ripe, toast 'n' butter jobs from California.

Sweet fortification
Some things smell so comforting that you almost don't need to drink them. Top of that list come sweet oloroso sherry and old Madeira, both of which are as unfashionable and utterly soothing as electric blankets and hot-water bottles.

Hot toddies
The Scots swear by this DIY antifreeze device. Take a generous helping of Scotch whisky, add some lemon juice, hot water, lemon slices, cloves, cinnamon and a couple of big spoonfuls of honey. Good for relieving aches, pains and colds.

Warm, mulled magic
Pour a bottle of red wine into a pan. Add cinnamon sticks, a dash of brandy, clove-studded oranges, and brown sugar. Heat all this without allowing it to reach boiling point. If you don't like wine, try making mulled cider by adding Calvados and slices of apple instead of brandy and oranges.

Cream liqueurs
In extreme emergencies, you might need to use the equivalent of an alcoholic milkshake. Liqueurs such as Baileys Irish Cream and Amarula deliver the perfect comfort combo of sweetness, silky textures and easy flavours.

Dark, oak-aged rums
For those living in cooler latitudes, there is nothing better than a bit of Caribbean aromatherapy to erase the winter blues. Brown sugar, coconut, spice, vanilla, caramel and coffee... the smell of good rum reads like an ingredient list for a good cake-baking session.

Barley wine
These strong, mahogany-coloured bottled beers have traditionally been drunk as winter warmers. With a strength that often reaches the same level as wine, and with flavours sometimes described as 'winey', you could say they are drinks with a split-personality disorder. Be warned, however. Drink more than a few glasses of this confused beer, and you'll most likely begin to feel pretty confused yourself.

...you be the one...

ATTRACTIVE TALL N/S MALE GSOH
in touch with emotional and sensitive side,
loves going to pubs, clubs and cinema
WLTM genuine attractive open minded
female for fun, friendship and romance.
Will you be the one to uncork my bottle?

Love booze

Booze and love are inextricably linked. The former uses the latter to market itself (although it seems to confuse love with sex most of the time), and the latter's path is strewn with the empty bottles of successful and failed courtship. As we have already seen, there are good and bad bottles to serve at a wedding, and alcohol can also play a crucial comforting role should the whole thing go belly up. Here, however, I am going to concentrate on those earlier stages of love, when choosing the right drink can be as important as remembering to floss and hiding the embarrassing parts of your CD collection.

Yes, folks, there are right and wrong ways to woo with drink. A bottle of chilled Cristal and a copy of *This is Spinal Tap* would be a good way to break the proverbial ice, whereas a cheap bottle of Asti and a Led Zepellin soundtrack will probably get you the ice bucket in your lap. Here, then, is my crash-course in booze and the fine art of seduction.

Beer, wine or spirits?
I know the Belgians will disagree with me on this, but beer is about as sexy as a V-neck sweater with patches sewn onto the elbows. It also makes you burp and go to the toilet a lot. Spirits (*see* 'Seductive or retro cocktails', page 164) are a good first-date anaesthetic, but you have to make sure that both parties are taking the same prescription, or embarrassment of some form is guaranteed. And wine – well, if you get it right, this is by far the best method of achieving that Barry White mood.

Some basic wine rules
The trick is to look like you've made an effort but without giving the impression that you are complete a wine geek. Reciting vintage charts, using a decanter, and thumbing through a Robert Parker wine guide will have the same effect as serving up kippers and bromide tea. Avoid clichés (a bottle of St-Amour will definitely get them running a mile), bizarre bottles brought back from holiday, and definitely don't bring out your dad's homemade wine.

Does size matter?

Unless it's a mega-expensive dessert wine, bringing out a half-bottle will definitely send out the wrong message, as will a magnum, which (if it's the bloke who brings it out) is like asking your date whether she wants to see your bright-red sports car with extra-wide wheels. Stick to normal-sized bottles.

Does expensive wine guarantee success?

There's a wonderful saying that goes: 'Money can't buy you happiness, but at least it will buy you a fancy car to go and look for it'. The same principle applies to booze. A great wine won't buy you love, but at least you'll have something nice to drink while you're trying to find it. Sadly, the world's sexiest wines do tend to be the most expensive, but always buy within your means, because love can be a long-haul ride. Going from Puligny on the first date to plonk on the fifth is not going to impress.

Ten sexy drinks

1 Right Bank Bordeaux (sweetly ripe, succulent Merlot)
2 Red burgundy (it's all in the silky texture)
3 Italian reds (stylish packaging, stylish wines)
4 Viognier (the sexiest-smelling wine in the world)
5 Vintage Champagne (trust me: it just works, okay?)
6 The Martini (warm, fuzzy glow guaranteed)
7 Rum (for a little tropical assistance)
8 Cream liqueurs (unfashionable, but very effective)
9 Sauternes (the greatest aphrodisiac ever created)
10 Australian Liqueur Muscat (one for the bedside table)

Ten turn-off drinks

1 Left Bank Bordeaux (too traditional and too hard to drink)
2 Port (too attached to the pipe and slippers)
3 Muscadet (too acidic)
4 Lager (too gassy)
5 Bag-in-box wine (too cheap)
6 Own-labels and big brands (too unimaginative)
7 Gin & Tonic (too colonial)
8 Pre-mixed cocktails (too lazy)
9 Rosé (too clichéd)
10 Homebrew (too undrinkable)

9

The
Three Tennants
in The Park

Row 1
Seat 112

£ 32.50
FULL
COUNTER

Alfresco booze

The Australians take outdoor drinking extremely seriously. They have drive-in bottle shops with refrigerators the size of barns, they use cool boxes that are built to withstand a direct nuclear hit (let alone a little sunshine) and they spend unlimited man hours in the quest to develop the very latest in insulated bottle-holders. If there were a 'keeping drinks cold' event in the Olympics, the Aussies would romp home with gold every time. Just like human beings, drinks begin to behave differently when you warm them up. Raising the temperature of a wine will tend to accentuate the alcohol and oak, so a big California Chardonnay will quickly taste like a flabby piece of wood with a sweet afterburn. Warmth will also make low-acid wines seem limp and structureless, so if you don't want something that feels as deflated as a punctured ego, go for a style of wine that has a bit of crunch from the start. Here are a few other suggestions to make parklife an enjoyable, rather than depressing, liquid blur.

FOUR PICNIC-RESISTANT WINE STYLES

1 AROMATIC WHITES To cope with all the competing whiffs of the great outdoors, it helps to go for something suitably extrovert in the nasal department. New Zealand Sauvignon Blanc, Argentine Torrontes or Hungarian Irsai Oliver are three you could smell even in a force-10 gale.

2 LOW-ALCOHOL, SLIGHTLY SWEET WHITES It might not be the most fashionable picnic wine, but an off-dry German Riesling is one of the hardiest when it comes to outdoor exposure.

3 SOFT, JUICY REDS If chilling is not an option, take reds rather than whites and go for the softest, most uncomplicated style on the shelf. Yup, there is a welcome home for Beaujolais after all.

4 FIZZY & FUN Moscato d'Asti is probably the best picnic wine going. Light in weight, gently fizzy, aromatic and with just enough sweetness to mask any

deficiencies caused by the heat, this stuff was made for the unprepared alfresco drinker.

FIVE SUMMER COCKTAILS THAT CAN BE MADE ON A RUG

To get around the ice problem, just make sure you put the spirits in the freezer the night before so at least one of the ingredients is really cold.

1 CUBA LIBRES White rum, cola, lime. Whoever said that a rum and Coke couldn't sound exotic?

2 MINT JULIPS Bourbon, 2 sugar cubes, mint. Crush some mint with the sugar and a dash of Bourbon. Top up with ice (if available) and Bourbon.

3 MOJITOS Rum, mint, lime, soda water. Mix some rum, a few sprigs of mint and some lime. Add sugar to taste and top up with soda water.

4 MOSCOW MULES Vodka, 1 lime, ginger beer. Squeeze some lime into a glass and pour the other two on top.

5 SEA BREEZES Vodka, cranberry, grapefruit juice. The balance should be about 3:1 in cranberry's favour.

KEEPING WINE COOL AT PICNICS

One of the drawbacks of taking to the open air is the distinct lack of public refrigerators in parks and picnic areas (maybe the authorities are concerned about the possibility of fridge rage), so you need to be prepared.

- COOL BOXES Fill with ice and bottles and use the melting cubes for your cocktails.
- EVAPORATION Wrap your wine in thin, wet cloths or newspaper and evaporation will cause a release of energy and a cooling effect on the bottle.
- FROZEN JACKETS Use some of those Rapid Ice sleeves designed to chill your wine. They act as good insulators as well, and should keep bottles cold for a couple of hours.
- FROZEN WINE Don't be afraid to super-chill your wine before venturing out. Wine will not be damaged by a quick stay in the freezer, but if you let it freeze completely you will find yourself with a broken bottle and Chardonnay sludge all over your frozen peas.
- RUNNING WATER A bottle will cool faster in running water even if the water isn't particularly cold.

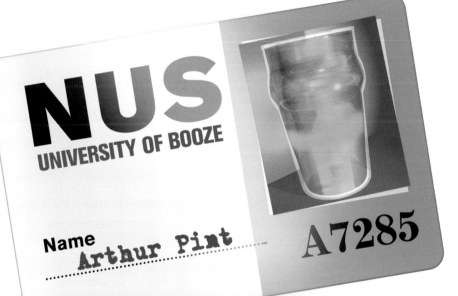

Student booze

One of the great intellectual challenges that the student faces – apart from how to get those four-hour loan books out of the library without alarms going off – is an understanding of the economics of booze. Fitting three years of hard entertaining into the sort of budget that would make even the Eritrean transport minister laugh might look like an impossible task, but by following some basic rules you can avoid resorting to lighter fuel. Here, then, is some practical advice you won't find in your university prospectus.

1 Choose a university in an economically challenged (ie, cheap) part of the country, and use the beer prices in the student-union bars to compile a short list. And if your chosen place of study happens to be near a border with another country, even better. A few weekend road trips and you'll have built up a good stash of duty-free contraband.

2 If at all possible, try to enrol at a university in a high-altitude city (Johannesburg and La Paz spring to mind). Alcohol takes effect far quicker in thin air, so your expenses will be substantially lower.

3 Buy a homebrew kit and turn your digs into a microbrewery. The only trouble is that you might need to start a coffee-grinding sideline just to disguise the smell of hops, malt and barley.

4 Become friends with a local restaurateur and offer to recycle the empties. Take home some well-known expensive labels, and when that important date comes around, just decant the contents of your bag-in-box into said classy receptacle and serve.

5 Buy all your booze in bulk in the New Year and summer sales. And if space doesn't permit that option, switch to plan B, which involves throwing loyalty cards out the window and becoming a ruthless supermarket promotion-hopper. Discounts, special offers, seven-for-six deals – you need never pay the full price for your favourite brand.

6 Becoming a master in round-avoidance (that strange practice of buying drinks for everyone) is essential if you are to survive financially. Try always to finish your drink when all your mates are still halfway through theirs, thus allowing you to offer a round in the safe knowledge that it will be turned down.

7 Plot a map of all the happy hours (they are rarely just an hour these days) in the local bars and organize your drinking time around them.

8 Apply for holiday work experience in wine shops and make the most of staff discounts and in-store tastings.

9 Learn how to disguise bad wine. For white wines, just switch the fridge to a lower temperature – flavours and aromas tend to become more suppressed the colder the wine gets – or use cassis to make a plonk-sweetening kir. For cheap red wine, you could either heat it up and turn it into a more palatable mulled wine, or make sure your diet is based on extremely spicy food.

10 Join the university wine-appreciation society.

CLASSIC STUDENT STAPLES

ABSINTHE The jolly green giant of the student party circuit.

CAVA Where would the student celebration be without this Spanish gift to the cheap fizz gods?

FABS Flavoured Alcoholic Beverages (or alcopops, as they were once known) are basically sweet cocktails packaged in an easy-to-grip lager bottle.

HAVANA CLUB RUM Cuba, Che Guevara... need we say more?

LAGER IN LARGE CANS You can always spot a student fridge by the number of tall, 25-percent-extra cans crammed into the veg rack.

RED WINES FROM EASTERN EUROPE Cheap, reliable and guaranteed to match any student food.

TEQUILA SLAMMERS The fast, effective way to forget that impending essay deadline.

VODKA & RED BULL The vodka gets you drunk and the Red Bull keeps you awake so you can get drunk even longer.

WINE BOXES Good value for money and they don't break when you knock them over.

Duty-free booze

Usually we buy booze because we need a drink or because we are preparing for a social event. But sometimes we buy it for no other reason than it is there in front of us and it happens to be cheap. The name of this type of booze is duty free. As you are reading this, millions of people all around the world are buying wine and spirits in crowded airport terminals, on ferries and ocean liners, at border crossings on land and while zooming across time zones at 30,000 feet. You can pick up a bottle of Mouton-Rothschild as you rush for your flight to Bangkok, or find a rare bottle of Scotch in places you'd never expect to come across one. And it's all thanks to an Irishman called Brendan O'Regan.

Just over 50 years ago, O'Regan helped set up the world's first duty-free airport shop in Shannon in the Republic of Ireland. In 1947, Shannon Airport – where transatlantic flights refuelled before flying on to Newfoundland – was classified as a 'free zone'. Seeing an opportunity to milk a wealthy American market, O'Regan began selling local spirits to transit passengers returning to the US. He sold Cork Gin for the equivalent of 44 pence a bottle and Irish whiskey for 53 pence and – not one to miss a financial opportunity – he even set up a lucrative mail-order service.

It wasn't long before other entrepreneurs got the same idea –

Alberto Motta set up a similar pioneering operation in Panama – and other airport authorities realized they were sitting on a retailing goldmine. By the 1970s, the arrival of jet aircraft and cheaper fares saw an explosion in the number of passengers and massive expansion in duty-free outlets. What had begun with booze quickly spread to tobacco, perfume, watches and jewellery, and before long, airport terminals began to resemble shopping malls.

Obviously, hand-luggage restrictions put a ceiling on how much you can buy – though one Thai family travelling first class once managed to take on board 11 cases of first-growth claret they'd bought at Berry Brothers in Heathrow – and the abolition of intra-EU duty-free is posing new challenges. Yet when so much money is at stake, a little bureaucracy is never going to be allowed to spoil the party. In some places, 'duty free' is being re-branded as 'travel retail', and operators are coming up with new ideas – exclusive products, purchase-on-arrival and home delivery being three examples – to keep passengers coming through the doors.

Apart from filling some time before your delayed plane takes off, is it worth buying duty-free booze? Financially, the answer has to be an immediate 'yes'. Back at Berry Brothers, you could save nearly £3,000 on a magnum of Château Pétrus; elsewhere, there are always good savings to be made on expensive premium spirits like single-malt whisky and Cognac. They key is to buy well-respected brands rather than gimmicky gift packs.

Duty-free exclusives
Walk around any decent airport duty-free shop and you'll find a lot of labels you've never seen before; products like Johnnie Walker Deco and Beefeater Crown Jewel can't be bought in your local high-street stores. Some drinks companies use duty free as a test market for new products (Camus, for instance, launched a new Cognac called Neon aimed at younger [female] drinkers) while others use limited releases and rare bottlings as duty-free exclusive carrots for label collectors.

Welcome to travel retail
You might think that the end of intra-European duty free would mean the end of booze bargains, but you'd be wrong. Many of the drinks operators in London's Heathrow are absorbing the VAT themselves and continue to offer prices that are either the same (or only marginally more) than before.

Good duty-free destinations
From my own bottle-clutching experiences, the best airports to be delayed in are Heathrow, Singapore, Brussels, Sydney (where you can buy on arrival), Istanbul and Hong Kong (both brand new), Dubai, Copenhagen and Rio.

Healthy booze

If current scientific opinion is to be believed, I must have the healthiest job in the world. Hardly a week goes by without the release of another piece of research showing that moderate drinking can be good for you. This might seem like novel news to those who have been brought up believing booze is bad, but the truth is, the benefits of the daily tipple have been recognized for a long time. If you were admitted to London's St Bartholomew's Hospital in the early 1800s, you'd have been allowed a daily allowance of three pints of beer a day and occasional doses of medicinal drinks called caudle and possett. Caudle was thin gruel mixed with ale or wine and spices, while possett was warm milk curdled with ale and sweetened with sugar. No wonder demand for hospital beds was so high.

Today, despite continued scepticism in countries such as the US, acceptance for the benefits of alcohol consumption has returned. It may be a while before wine labels carry the message 'a couple of glasses a day can reduce the risk of heart attacks, diabetes and Alzheimer's disease', but evidence is stacking up to a level that can't be ignored.

What is 'drinking in moderation'?
In an effort to quantify the unquantifiable, those nice people whose job it is to try and define moderation have come up with sensible-drinking guidelines. In the UK, these are three to four units of alcohol per day if you are a man, two to three units per day if you are a woman. If you are using large (250ml or 8fl oz) glasses and you are drinking an average 12.5 percent abv claret, this equates to 1.25 and 0.93 glasses, respectively.

The problem with all this (apart from the fact the levels seem worryingly low) is obvious. There's no such thing as a standard person, alcohol levels vary enormously from wine to wine and drink to drink, and there are big differences between drinking with food and quaffing with conversation. The best advice is to drink small amounts regularly rather than large amounts erratically.

MYTHS AND REALITIES OF THE HEALTHY BAR MENU

GUINNESS IS GOOD FOR YOU There might be a bit of extra iron content in there and the live yeast in the bottle-conditioned version is thought to act as a good laxative. But good for you? Give me another pint and I'll think about it.

A PINT OF MILK STOUT WILL HELP YOU GET ABOUT Milk stouts contain milk sugars and have traditionally been served to invalids. Whether an extra dose of carbohydrates and calories comes under the definition of healthy is, however, debatable.

UNFILTERED WHEAT BEER IS GOOD FOR THE SKIN Some people reckon the vitamins in these yeasty beers are good for the complexion. I'm unconvinced, but who cares when they taste this good?

A WEE DRAM OF WHISKY IS GOOD FOR THE BLOOD Reports in several UK medical journals have pointed out that Scotch malt whisky contains the same polyphenols that are found in red wine, and thus maintain that it can help increase the amount of good, cardio-protective cholesterol in the blood.

CHILEAN RED WINE IS THE HEALTHIEST WINE ON THE BLOCK Research at Glasgow University has revealed that Chilean Cabernet Sauvignon seems to have higher levels of flavonols (antioxidants) than red wines from other countries. Scientists believe it could be related to the high levels of bright sunlight that are present in Chilean vineyards.

HOPPY BEERS ARE GOOD FOR THE HEART American studies have found that hops contain a chemical called xanthohumol that is six times more effective than antioxidants found in citrus fruits. Unfortunately, you'd have to drink 800 pints a day to gain any beneficial effects.

MUSCADET IS GOOD FOR CELLULITE AND CHAMPAGNE IS GOOD FOR DEPRESSION Frenchman Dr Emeric Maury believes traces of minerals found in wines act like homeopathic remedies. According to Maury (I like this guy), Beaujolais helps prevent sore throats, Cabernet Sauvignon helps protect against food poisoning, and Valpolicella is recommended for its anti-inflammatory properties. Sign me up for Dr Maury's therapy programme.

The home booze kit

In the freezer

I reckon you can tell a lot about someone by simply poking your nose in their freezer. If you find an eclectic range of spirits and a row of frozen shot glasses, then clearly they take their drinking seriously. If, however, there is nothing but an ice tray and an old packet of frozen peas, the chances of you being offered a decent drink are slim. The minimum freezer requirement is one decent bottle of vodka and one of those Rapid Ice sleeves for chilling wine quickly.

In the fridge

The fridge should be treated like a survival kit for future drinking situations. A bottle of Bloody Mary mix should always be on hand, as should bottles of Tabasco and Worcestershire sauce (the last two don't need to be in the fridge). A bottle of Angostura bitters is an important cocktail ingredient and a good stomach tonic as well. Other permanent fridge residents include a bottle of Champagne (unexpected celebrations and dates), six bottles of real German lager (no Sol, Bud, or XXXX, please), a couple of bottles of New World Chardonnay (for the post-work comfort drink) and some cranberry juice (a token healthy gesture). Food is an optional extra.

On the bookshelf

THE BEST BEGINNER'S WINE BOOK
Essential Winetasting by Michael Schuster (Mitchell Beazley) is the most practical guide I know for helping the wine virgin lose his or her cherry and find their blackcurrants and strawberries.

THE BEST A–Z OF WINE KNOWLEDGE
The Oxford Companion to Wine (Oxford University Press) is a fantastic reference guide and excellent doorstop.

THE BEST INVESTMENT GUIDE
Get yourself a subscription to Robert Parker's *Wine Advocate*.

THE ONE BEER BOOK WORTH BUYING
Michael Jackson's *Beer Companion* (Mitchell Beazley) takes you on a comprehensive crawl through the major (and obscure) beer styles of the world.

THE BEST GUIDE TO THE STRONG STUFF *Spirits and Cocktails* by Dave Broom (Carlton) will get you from absinthe to zubrowka and every distilled destination in between.

Wine glasses

If you believe a certain Austrian glass manufacturer called Georg Riedel, your kitchen should be filled with enough different stemware to set up your own glass-pinging orchestra. According to Riedel, every style of wine requires a particular shape of glass in order to maximize its aromatic potential and direct its subtle nuances to the correct part of the tongue. Yes, well, all that is fine if budget and storage space are equally unlimited and if you prefer to scrutinize rather than drink your wine. But for the rest of us, just one decent set will suffice. A basic tulip-shaped glass with enough interior space for a good swirl is all you need, whether you're drinking Jacob's Creek or Pétrus.

A decanter

This isn't an essential item (an ordinary jug will do), but a decanter does come in handy when you want to serve guests a wine without them knowing how little you spent. And then when you can afford some decent gear, giving your wine a little pre-dinner airing will allow it to perform cartwheels rather than just forward rolls.

A good-quality corkscrew

The classic waiter's corkscrew (called 'the waiter's friend') is still my favourite de-corking utensil because a) it can deal with everything from plastic corks to delicate bits of Portuguese bark, and b) you can open beer bottles with it, too. For weak wrists, the Screwpull brand of corkscrew is the most efficient and easy to use – even your granny will be able to perform sommelier duties with one of these. And top of the list of avoidables is the ubiquitous 'butterfly' model (the one with two arms that are pulled down), which will do its very best to help you not get the cork out.

A big cool box

Buying one of those big, insulated drinks containers might seem like a daft decision in the January sales, but when summer comes, you will be prepared for outdoor drinking.

A blender

An essential domestic accessory for making fruit pureés (for cocktails) and smoothies. It can also be used to help soften young, tannic wines that need a good dose of vigorous aeration. (Yes, I've tried it.)

Hangover cures

First of all, let's get one thing straight: there's no such thing as a hangover cure! Drink too much alcohol and there's good chance you'll end up feeling and looking like Keanu Reeves in that gooey, baldy-head scene in *The Matrix* – you know, the one where he wakes up from his coma and finds the shocking reality of his real existence? And like Keanu, you, too, will feel like pulling out the cord from the back of your head and sliding down a watery chute into the safe arms of a big, cool dude called Morpheus. In the likely event that Laurence Fishburne is unavailable, one or more of the following remedies might help ease the pain.

Hair of the dog that bit you

The most popular way of dealing with the after-effects of over-indulgence is to simply admit defeat and indulge again. Drinks such as the Bloody Mary (add vodka to the Virgin Mary in the healthy cocktails section) and the Corpse Reviver (Cognac, orange juice, Champagne, and a few drops of pastis) will make you feel better in the short term, but it is just a delaying tactic.

The big breakfast

Referred to in Britain as the 'greasy-spoon breakfast', this full medley of fried sausage, bacon, egg, bread and anything else that can feasibly be cooked in a frying pan might soothe the munchies, but don't bank on your headache disappearing. You could also try a Prairie Oyster (one egg yolk, a dash of olive oil, dashes of Tabasco and Worcestershire sauces, a few drops of lemon juice and pepper and salt), but have a bucket handy.

Fruit smoothies

If you want something that tastes comforting, is easy to swallow and scores high on the goodness front, a glass of blended fruit, yoghurt and honey is a good option. Choose fruits that have a lot of vitamin C in them and don't put so much banana in that pulling it through a straw requires industrial powers of suction.

Oral electrolyte powders

We all know that the worst symptoms of a hangover are caused by a certain mistress of morning misery known as Dee Hydration, so it doesn't take a huge leap of logic to work out that rehydration remedies might be the best cure of all. Go to your nearest pharmacy and ask for a packet of Dioralyte – it's for diarrhoea, not hangovers, but trust me on this. Dissolved in water, this remedy helps restore the balance of sugars, salts and fluids in your body.

Short, sharp shock treatment

There's nothing like a dose of nerve-shredding fear and a burst of adrenaline to help remove all thoughts of having a bad-head day. Jumping into an icy lake (a Scandinavian favourite), running down a Spanish street with a large, angry bull threatening to impale you from behind or being told you are about to get married in one hour's time... any of these usually helps a hangover miraculously disappear in seconds.

Exercise

Sweating out all the toxins from your body is sound in principle, but there is always a chance that in your weakened state, you'll collapse from the effort. Swimming is a good idea because you can stay horizontal and the water supports you.

Stay right where you are

Perhaps the best cure of all is to stay in bed until the hangover goes away. This does require that you keep a good supply of water near your bed and that you can master the art of using a bed pan.

Hangover reduction

Total avoidance is almost impossible, but there are a few things you can do that will help set the headache volume level at two instead of 11.

1 Eat something before or while you drink.

2 Stick to spirits such as vodka rather than whisky, and try not to treat the bar as some sort of DJ mixing desk. Dubbing some grain over some grape and cutting in some liqueur loops over the top is a recipe for the shakes, rocks and rolls.

3 Avoid cheap red wine. If you suffer adverse reactions to sulphur, stick to organic wines.

4 Alternate your alcohol consumption with glasses of water. Unfortunately, this means that you spend most of the evening in the toilet, but also that you won't spend the next day regretting the night before.

Booze blurb

BEER

BOTTLE-CONDITIONED BEER A beer that is bottled with a small dose of yeast and sugar so that it re-ferments in the bottle.

BOOZER The slang name for a pub.

GASTROPUB A new style of pub that is renowned as much for its food and wine as it is for its beer.

LIQUOR In some circles, this is a generic term for alcohol (with 'hard liquor' meaning spirits), but in the brewing world, liquor means water.

MASH The name for the mixture of grain and water that is fermented to create beer.

MICROBREWERY A small brewery.

PUB The short word for Public House, the place where British people go to drink beer.

REAL ALE A beer that ferments in the container in which it is served (either cask or bottle) and which is served without additional gas.

ZYMURGY The artful science of brewing.

SPIRITS & COCKTAILS

CONGENERS Chemical compounds found in spirits thought to contribute to hangovers.

HEADS, HEARTS AND TAILS The respective names for the first, middle and last parts of the distillate that comes out of a still.

JIGGER A small glass used to measure out shots of spirit.

MIXOLOGIST Poncey name for a cocktail barman.

MUDDLING Barman's term for mixing/crushing fruit or herbs to be used in a cocktail.

PROOF A term used to indicate alcoholic strength.

SHOOTER Spirit-based drinks (served in shot glasses) that are drunk in one gulp.

SHOT A single measure of spirit (generally 25ml in UK bars, 1–1.5ozs in the US).

SPEED RAIL The rack of 'house' spirits that bartenders use if no specific brand is ordered.

WINE

APPELLATION A geographically defined wine region.

BARRELS/BARRIQUES Hollow oak containers in which wine is stored and left to mature.

BASKET-PRESSED A wine made from grapes that have been squeezed in an old, wooden, cylindrical press.

CHIPS Small pieces of oak wrapped in a muslin bag and dunked in a tank of wine to add oak flavour.

COLD-FERMENTED WINE A (white) wine made by fermenting grape juice at very low temperatures to keep as much fresh-fruit flavour as possible.

COMPLEX Wine-tasting term that refers to wine with a multi-dimensional personality.

GOOD NOSE Means a wine has some nice aromatic qualities.

LEFT ON ITS LEES Lees is the word used for the dead yeast cells that fall to the bottom of the tank/barrel after fermentation. 'Left on its lees' means the wine has been left in contact with this sediment in order to pick up some interesting flavours.

MALOLACTIC FERMENTATION A process that converts hard, malic acid in a wine into softer, creamier-tasting lactic acid.

NEW WORLD Generally refers to all winemaking countries in the southern hemisphere (and the US).

OLD WORLD Ditto the northern hemisphere (minus the US).

ON THE PALATE Wine-tasting term that simply means 'in the mouth'.

SINGLE-ESTATE/VINEYARD/BLOCK/ROW A label term that indicates the wine has been made from a specific area of vines. It is not a guarantee of higher quality.

STAVES Oak planks that are suspended in a tank of wine to add oaky flavours.

TERROIR The combination of physical factors (climate, soil, slope, etc) that help make each wine taste slightly different.

THE FINISH A tasting expression that refers to the length of a wine's aftertaste.

VARIETAL WINE A wine made from a single grape variety.

VINTAGE Another word for harvest or year. A vintage wine means absolutely nothing at all except that the wine has been made from the harvest of a particular year.

WILD FERMENT Fermentation using indigenous (wild) rather than cultured yeast.

GENERAL

DADS Designer Alcoholic Drinks.

DUTY FREE A term applied to alcohol sold in airports, at land borders, on ferries, etc, where excise duty (tax) does not have to be paid.

FABS Flavoured Alcoholic Beverages (otherwise known as alcopops).

RTDS Ready to Drink (another term for FABs).

Index

Index

Acknowledgements

This book would have remained an unfermented idea had it not been for the vision, enthusiasm and belief of Margaret Little. Cheers, Margaret: thanks for making it happen, and I hope the end result is close to what you had in mind back at that first wine-fuelled conversation. A big thank-you, too, to Hilary Lumsden for manning the taps on a day-to-day basis and for putting up with the mood swings of the stressed-out landlord. To all the rest of the bar staff at Cassell – thanks for putting in all those hours of overtime. A large toast to David Eldridge, whose superb illustrations have put an inspired garnish on what would otherwise be a very ordinary-looking cocktail of copy. To Jamie Terrell for putting in a lot of hard work on the cocktail section and for being there with a drink when I needed it. Thanks to Simon and all the gang at Class. And finally, the biggest thanks go to my family and friends, whose love and understanding helped keep Booze flowing from start to finish.